90 MINUTES IN HEAVEN

90 MINUTES IN HEAVEN

SEE LIFE'S TROUBLES
IN A WHOLE NEW LIGHT

DON PIPER

WORTHY
RESOURCES

CONTENTS

INTRODUCTION

*"And this is the testimony: that God has given us eternal life,
and this life is in His Son."*

— 1 John 5:11 (NKJV)

The first thing I usually say is that this is a testimony. It's not a sermon; it's not a message; it's a testimony, and I think that's very important. I feel like we don't do testimonies as much as we should.

I also want to issue a caveat: people will sometimes read a book or listen to a story like mine and think, *Gee, mine isn't nearly as compelling as that. I wasn't killed in a car wreck; I didn't see heaven.* Maybe they have been raised in the church, been faithful members all their lives, and led a fairly trouble-free life, and so they assume that excludes their testimony from being told.

I believe quite the contrary. You don't have to live like the devil to have a good testimony; your story is important and you should share it. That's why I was convinced to share mine even though I really didn't plan to.

Through the course of this study I'll be sharing my experience, and through the daily lessons you'll have the opportunity to tell yours. May the scriptures you study and the thoughts you ponder prepare your heart for the heaven that's being prepared for you!

— *Don Piper*

HEAVEN IN THE NEXT INSTANT?

"You have decided the length of our lives. You know how many months we will

live, and we are not given a minute longer." — Job 14:5 (NLT)

How I Died and Lived to Tell About It

Shortly after I left a ministerial conference in East Texas to return home to Houston, an eighteen-wheeler veered into my lane and hit my car head-on. The EMTs pronounced me dead on the scene. Instantly upon impact, I found myself in heaven, a place of indescribable beauty, love, reunion, glorious music, perfection, and ecstasy. I'll tell you more about that later.

Minutes later, another pastor who had been at the conference, Dick Onerecker, arrived at the scene; he stopped, wanting to pray for the injured. The medics told him I was dead, but Dick still felt a strong urging from God, so he crawled into what remained of the car, put his hand on my shoulder, and prayed. After a while he began to sing a hymn, and to his great surprise, I began to sing with him.

Dick convinced the incredulous EMTs to come to the car. They found a pulse and rushed me from hospital to hospital to keep me alive until they finally reached Hermann Hospital in Houston, six and a half hours after the accident. Word went out to churches everywhere, and thousands of Christians began interceding for my life.

My injuries were extensive and critical, to say the least. Large hunks of bone were missing from my leg and arm, and doctors feared those limbs were beyond saving. But a new device designed to stimulate bone regrowth—the Ilizarov frame—had recently been approved for use in the U.S. The process promised to be long and painful, but because I was unconscious, my wife made the decision to apply the device.

I endured a grueling two-year recovery, including thirteen months in the hospital and thirty-four operations. Often I prayed that God would take me back to heaven. When that didn't happen, I grew despondent because I could find no meaning in seemingly endless months of suffering.

But eventually I did find meaning, thanks to the help of a friend. Even more, I found new purpose for my life and a ministry that has become my mission and passion. Thousands have been helped by my testimony about heaven, and have turned to God's Word because of it—which is where this study will be focused.

Coming to Terms with Reality

Almost all of us have some sort of outline for the story of our life, with certain elements in common: a satisfying career, a good education, a happy marriage, obedient children, a nice home, money in the bank, adorable grandchildren, and a comfortable retirement.

I was no exception. I was thirty-eight years old and in good health with my future set. My story was moving along according to plan. When I left that conference in East Texas, I had no idea that my world was about to be smashed into chaos.

While my experience after that collision was unique in one way—few people who die and go to heaven come back to tell about it—in other ways, it is common to just about everyone. Life isn't obligated to follow our outline. We make decisions, large and small, which we think will lead to one result but which often lead instead to something utterly unexpected. When I decided to take a new route home that day, little did I know how far-reaching the results would be.

We sometimes make other, less-innocent decisions that lead to grave consequences, such as Adam and Eve's choice in the Garden of Eden. God's gift of freedom to make decisions is a tremendous one. But at the same time, He has placed us in a position of high responsibility where everything we do has wide ramifications in our work, our relationships, our worship. We exercise our God-given responsibility in these areas by making decisions, and God gives us great leeway in making them—even to the point of allowing us to occasionally make disastrous choices.

Even if we do habitually seek God's wisdom so as to avoid most self-imposed consequences, occasionally we are victims of plot spoilers beyond our control—some caused by the choices of others and some by acts of nature. Accidents, diseases, divorces, job losses, family deaths, financial ruin—eventually everyone runs up against such unexpected twists. Obviously, Christians are not exempt from the effects of evil. We face the same uncertainties about the next minute as unbelievers.

I used to think it was a cliché to say that life is uncertain, but now I think we don't say it enough. No matter how detailed our plans, how lofty our dreams, or how elaborate the structures of our lives, at any moment those plans can be scrambled, those dreams can collapse, and construction on our life project can grind to a halt. Too many people, however, are living as if they don't believe it. But it's true; I can literally feel it in my bones!

The biggest plot spoiler of them all, of course, is death. It awaits everyone, lurking around some unknown corner, ready to ambush you and end your story, often long before you would prefer to conclude the chapters. And that is why we fear it: since Enoch and Elijah, the death rate among humans has been 100 percent. A quarter million people leave this planet every day, with every one of us a guaranteed future customer at the local mortuary.

In the face of our fear, it would be easy to just throw up our hands and say, "What's the use in trying if life is so uncertain that no endeavor is assured of completion?" But we who trust God and submit to Him will work to fulfill our calling and accomplish His will on earth, not because we expect to finish all we set out to do, but because God wants to see us in action as if the earth were not under the curse of the Fall. As the parable of the talents (Matthew 25:14–30) illustrates, when we plan and work in spite of life's uncertainty, we are demonstrating our willingness to be what we were created to be—God's agents, bearing His Spirit, accepting His grace, and diligently going about His business. In return, God gives us assurance of heaven. His promise of a certain eternity is the antidote to despair, providing hope, meaning, and joy to an uncertain today.

So instead of viewing our lives as a futile quest, or pushing thoughts of our mortality aside as too dreadful to think about, we should prepare for what's to come just as one prepares for surgery to cure a life-threatening disease. You and I suffer from the fatal tumor of sin, and the Master Surgeon stands ready to cut it away and restore us to perfection. Doesn't it make sense to prepare for *that* operation in the same way we would prepare for one at our local hospital? Shouldn't we follow the Surgeon's directives so that when the time comes, we'll be ready?

Death certainly isn't good. It was inflicted on us by our archenemy Satan. God hates it. Christ wept over it. Paul calls it an enemy. Yet because of Christ's sacrifice and resurrection, the curse of death has been transformed. Death still strikes, but its poison is no longer deadly. Thanks to Christ, it not only frees us from the suffering and uncertainties of this life, but it is now our passageway to new life in heaven, where we will spend eternity in the presence of God. This is why the apostle Paul anticipated death and even yearned for it (2 Corinthians 5:8–9). If we focus on the cure—the new life—it will help us overcome our fear of the surgical process itself.

I find it significant that all cultures in history have believed in some sort of afterlife. God has planted the idea in the human consciousness and given every person an innate desire to be with Him after death. Without Jesus and salvation, heaven becomes a mere wish for the future, but for believers it is a surety.

The Bible affirms the validity of this belief and gives us tantalizing hints of the nature of paradise. And I can personally attest to the reality of heaven's splendor. In fact, my vivid experience in heaven is one of the things that snapped me out of my apprehension. I *know* heaven is real because I've tasted its wonders. Now I am eager to return, and that longing—along with wanting to escape the pain and suffering I've endured throughout my long recovery—has obliterated all fear of death.

Being convinced of heaven is not only the most effective way to cope with the plot spoilers we must endure in our personal stories, but it gives us enormous power to live in this present world. My assurance of heaven has given me a new ministry and a new purpose. In fact, I'm convinced that this is why God sent me back. When I left my hospital bed thirteen months after the accident, excruciating pain and memories of heaven are the two things I carried with me that motivated me to communicate hope to suffering people. This ability to bless others is how my anticipation of heaven gives me power to live now.

Conviction of heaven can also give us power over a long list of things that often tempt us to spoil our own stories—fads and fashions, conformity with cultural values, peer pressure, lust, and materialism. These temptations won't affect a person with a strong assurance of heaven any more than a quick hot dog would tempt a person who knows a steak dinner with all the trimmings awaits at home.

Some people wonder, though, if achieving a good life now is more important than anticipating heaven. Isn't it wrong to emphasize a future in heaven, they ask, when we have a society to improve and a planet to save here and now? Doesn't heavenly mindedness selfishly put the focus on personal reward rather than the good of humankind?

Yes, it's mercenary to seek a self-serving reward, but not a reward appropriate to our legitimate endeavors. The proper reward for hard work is a nice paycheck. The proper reward for diligent studies is a good grade. The proper reward for a Christian is to hear "welcome home" from the smiling lips of our Father.

And it's true that we are charged to do our best to improve our world; Jesus urged us to become its preserving salt and guiding light. It's also true that some Christians seem to be so eternally minded that they are of no earthly good. But Christians are right to emphasize heaven. Anticipation of it saturates the pages of the New Testament and the writings of the early Christian fathers. They spoke of it, wrote of it, longed for it. And that anticipation gave them power to live their present lives joyfully, without fear of the unexpected.

Heaven made them bold and courageous. Death might be imminent, but it was not permanent, and they knew a better world awaited—a world free of all suffering, free of all fear, and free of

5

death. A world where no story ever ends.

That is what my experience has taught me as well. I have been shown that heaven is real, but the reality of heaven doesn't matter if you're not going. So, in this study, I invite you to come along. I want to help you get there, and I want to help you *want* to get there. I want to show you that you can have a better life here if heaven becomes a firm reality to you.

1. People change, and so do their stories. As a child, what did you want to be when you grew up? What are some of the unexpected turns your life has taken?

2. Have you ever been in a situation where you thought you were about to die? How did that experience affect you at the time? What about now?

3. Read James 5:16. Obviously, God could have revived Don without Dick Onerecker's prayer. So why did God have Dick pray for Don?

4. Though He loves us and cares about our well-being, God gives us no assurance of mortal life past the present moment. Why do you think that is?

5. Look up James 4:14. How does the temporary, uncertain nature of life affect your attitude toward the present and your thinking about the future?

6. Reflect on what Jesus said in Matthew 6:33–34 and respond.

   The top priorities in my life, in descending order, are:

   Of these priorities, the one to which I would sacrifice all others is:

LIVE WHAT YOU'VE LEARNED

In seventeenth-century England, it was customary for the church to toll a funeral bell for the death of a Christian. John Donne famously wrote, "Ask not for whom the bell tolls; it tolls for thee." Today, as an exercise in acclimatizing yourself to the certainty of death, every time you hear a bell or buzzer—be that a phone, church chimes, a computer notification, an elevator stopping, or a doorbell—think of it as Donne's bell tolling for you. Then stop for a moment and utter a prayer of thanks to God that He has transformed death from a grave into a passage.

DAY 1

LIFE IS UNCERTAIN, BUT GOD IS NOT

"Moreover, no man knows when his hour will come: As fish are caught in a cruel net, or birds are taken in a snare, so men are trapped by evil times that fall unexpectedly upon them."
— Ecclesiastes 9:12 (NIV)

Early in 2009 Pastor Fred Winters of First Baptist Church in Maryville, Illinois, invited me to speak to his congregation about heaven. I consented, and we set a date. But on a Sunday in March, a young man entered the church while Pastor Winters was preaching, walked up the center aisle, drew a .45-caliber handgun, and opened fire. Three bullets entered Pastor Winters' chest. He died from his wounds.

When Pastor Winters called me, little did he know that God would soon call *him*. He would experience heaven before I arrived to speak on it.

No doubt he fully expected to eat lunch with his family or friends after that morning's services. He had a calendar filled with appointments and plans. But none of it was to be.

Such is the house of cards that we live in. Frankly, I don't see how unbelievers can stand it. What keeps them from despair when they are trapped in a world where no plan is assured of completion, no effort is guaranteed results, and no relationship is lasting? As John Updike put it, "If this physical world is all, then it is a closed hell in which we are . . . condemned to watch other prisoners being slain."

Thankfully, as Christ followers, we know that the problems, pains, losses, and tragedies we encounter in this fallen world are not the end of our story. We can bear the burdens of this life with patience because we are assured of a future Home where none of these blights can ever again touch us.

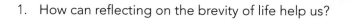

1. How can reflecting on the brevity of life help us?

2. Read Psalm 39:4–5, James 4:14, and 1 Peter 1:24. How should life's uncertainty affect your present outlook? Your future plans?

3. How should we live, according to 1 Peter 1:17? How can we do that?

4. Compare Psalm 90:12 with what King Hezekiah was told in 2 Kings 20:1. What attitude do these verses encourage us to adopt?

For a small reward,

a man will hurry

away on a long

journey; while for

eternal life, many

will hardly take a

single step.

—

Thomas á Kempis

Father, I thank You for the promise and assurance of heaven. Grant me, I pray, the wisdom to pursue what is eternal.

DAY 2

DEATH IS CERTAIN, BUT IT'S NOT PERMANENT

"Like water spilled on the ground, which cannot be recovered, so we must die. But God does not take away life; instead, he devises ways so that a banished person may not remain estranged from him." — 2 Samuel 14:14 (NIV)

When I was thirteen years old, my grandmother died. She was buried in Arkansas at a rural cemetery behind an aged, white clapboard church. On the walk toward the gravesite after the funeral, I noticed a cluster of Piper family tombstones. Suddenly my eyes were riveted by one in particular; it bore the inscription *Larry Donald Piper*. That is *my* name.

In shock I stopped, utterly stunned. I couldn't move. All I could do was stare at that tombstone with my name etched on it.

Moments later, my Aunt Maxine came along and gently urged me to head toward the burial site, but I just stood there. Perplexed, she followed my gaze to the stone and immediately understood. "Don," she said, "that's not *your* stone. Your Aunt Mildred had a little boy who died at birth, and he had exactly the same name as you. This is where he is buried."

Though a great relief settled over me in that moment, my name as I saw it that day is still engraved on my mind, reminding me that someday there will be a funeral for *this* Don Piper. We would all be wise to hold in our minds the image of a tombstone with our name on it, because nothing is more certain in this life than death.

Is it morbid to think like this? Not at all. Death is an unalterable reality, and the sooner we come to terms with it, the less anxious we'll be. Just remember, death is not the final word. Thanks to Christ, it is only the final leg on the Christian's journey toward Home.

1. What would your life be like if you thought death was permanent? How would you find meaning?

2. In what ways have you found the words of Job 1:21 to be true?

3. According to 1 Corinthians 15:54–55 and Hebrews 2:14–15, what has been destroyed?

5. What does 2 Timothy 1:10 say that believers have received? Do you usually treat this as news worth telling or as a secret worth keeping?

In my travels,

I have found that

those who keep

heaven in view

remain serene and

cheerful in the

darkest day.

—

Billy Graham

Father, when my faith grows weak and I am tempted to fall into fear, help me to remember that death and its power over me have been defeated forever.

11

DAY 3

THE POWER OF ANTICIPATING HEAVEN

"Since, then, you have been raised with Christ, set your hearts on things above, where Christ is seated at the right hand of God. Set your minds on things above, not on earthly things."
— Colossians 3:1–2 (NIV)

When I was a child and my parents told us kids that we were going to Grandma's house, we got so excited we'd jump about, clap, and squeal in anticipation. Years later, I remember telling my own children that we were taking them to Disney World. My son Joe could hardly wait. He counted the days and often reminded me of my promise—as if I would forget! He didn't realize that I was as eager to go as he was.

If Christians really understood what was awaiting them in heaven, they would anticipate their future destination in the same way. During my painful recovery from the accident, I could think of little else. Those ninety minutes I spent in heaven were so joyful and glorious that I couldn't understand why God sent me back to endure over a year of lying flat on my back while needles poked me, tubes fed and emptied me, scalpels sliced me, machines stretched me, and medical professionals poked, prodded, and patched me. Who wouldn't anticipate heaven under such hellish conditions! Yet even now that I'm recovered, with my pain manageable and my abilities restored to somewhat normal function, I still anticipate heaven just as strongly as I did in that hospital.

Heaven is more than a relief from suffering or a mere reward. It's finally arriving at the place we are meant to be, where we can continue to serve God and carry out His work with no impediments, no frustration, no conflict, and no pain—but with unlimited joy.

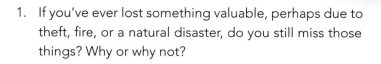

1. If you've ever lost something valuable, perhaps due to theft, fire, or a natural disaster, do you still miss those things? Why or why not?

2. If heaven awaits, what else ceases to be important, and why? See 2 Corinthians 5:1.

3. What did Jesus say is God's will for our lives in John 6:40?

4. Read Paul's honest words in Philippians 1:21–24. What's your preference? What would be hardest for you to leave behind? What would you gladly escape?

Each day brings us closer to death. If your treasures are on earth, that means each day brings you closer to losing your treasures.

—

Randy Alcorn

Father, please increase my awareness of both Your presence in my life and the home awaiting me in heaven.

DAY 4

DECISIONS THAT SHAPE ETERNITY

"Now listen, you who say, 'Today or tomorrow we will go to this or that city, spend a year there, carry on business and make money.' Why, you do not even know what will happen tomorrow." — James 4:13–14 (NIV)

When I think back on my accident, I am amazed at how many ultimately crucial decisions were made by various individuals. Here's a sampling of the more obvious ones.

When I got in my car, I decided to buckle my seat belt, which I often forgot to do.

Dick Onerecker and his wife left the conference before I did, but they decided to stop for coffee, which put them behind me. God instructed Dick to pray for me, but praying for the dead didn't exactly mesh with his theology. Deciding obedience should trump theology, he prayed anyway.

Years earlier in Russia, a brilliant doctor named Ilizarov invented a device to lengthen bones and ultimately decided to get his device approved in the U.S. Just weeks before my accident, a Houston physician decided to study the Ilizarov literature and learn of its possibilities, even though the device had never been used in the States. Later, while I lay unconscious, Dr. Greider presented the Ilizarov option to my wife, and she decided to have the device applied to my shattered leg and arm, thus saving both limbs.

These and other decisions contributed both to the accident and its outcome. All of our decisions—not just the major ones—are like ripples in a stream, affecting not only the present but eternity as well. Though we will never know the effect of our decisions, we can be sure that each one is crucial. Too crucial to make without God's guidance.

1. When faced with a difficult decision, who do you turn to for advice? Why do you trust them?

2. Where should we start if we want to live with eternity in mind? See 1 Corinthians 3:11–14.

3. If you made the same pledge as that of Joshua 24:15, how would it change your life?

4. What choice does Jesus describe in Matthew 7:13–14? What makes it hard?

5. What reassurance does Psalm 37:23–24 offer about making decisions?

A continual looking forward to the eternal world is not a form of escapism or wishful thinking, but one of the things a Christian is meant to do.

—

C. S. Lewis

Lord, help me make each choice under the guidance of Your Spirit and then place the result in Your trustworthy hands.

DAY 5

FINDING PURPOSE IN SUFFERING

"For our light and momentary troubles are achieving for us an eternal glory that far outweighs them all."
— 2 Corinthians 4:17 (NIV)

As I lay painfully incapacitated in my hospital bed, I knew I would never be normal again. And I wanted out of this life. Attached to tangles of tubes and beeping monitors, with glorious memories of heaven flooding my mind, I pleaded, "Take me back, God. *Please*."

But God did not take me back to heaven, and I wondered *why*. What was the point of it all? Thanks to the prayers, encouragement—and occasional chastisement—of good friends and medical professionals, I finally left the hospital with a better attitude. But the real turning point came years later when my friend David Gentiles showed me the purpose of my experiences. "You must share your story," he said. "Don't you realize what a powerful encouragement you can be to others?"

David's words penetrated straight to my heart. I had been so focused on myself that I hadn't thought about anyone else. Now I tell my story to everyone who asks, trusting that God will use my experiences to offer people assurance of heaven and a way to come through their suffering.

Telling my story has become my primary ministry. Telling your story would minister to others too. You may not think your story is dramatic or interesting, but you have endured circumstances that someone needs to hear. And your experiences with suffering have the same ultimate purpose as mine: helping others to get to heaven. I am convinced that this is why any of us are still here. We're here to help others arrive at their eternal destination; we are reservation agents for heaven.

1. Does having a reason for suffering help us endure? How?

2. What was Peter's admonition to those who are suffering in 1 Peter 4:19?

3. Read 1 Peter 2:9. Who are we, and what business should we be about?

4. How does Ecclesiastes 9:10 say we should face whatever happens today?

5. If you have ever endured serious pain or trauma, list the good things that came from it. Have you shared this experience with others?

He whose head is in heaven need not fear to put his feet into the grave.

—

Matthew Henry

Lord, please teach me pain's purpose in my life so that I may give hope to those who think it has passed them by.

17

DOES GOD STILL WORK IN MIRACULOUS WAYS?

"And he that sat upon the throne said, Behold, I make all things new."

— Revelation 21:5a (KJV)

Why I Believe in Miracles

The Bible is filled with miracles, many of them spectacular and performed in front of witnesses—seas parting, manna falling, plagues descending, donkeys talking, even people raised from the dead. Most Christians I know believe these events occurred, but I run across some who think that when the Bible was finished, all miracles ceased.

Not long ago I spoke for four days at a church in Alaska. I was surprised to find that the music minister's voice was little more than a croak, and I wondered why a man with such a poor voice would be chosen for that position. I soon learned that he had been a victim of throat cancer, which ruined his voice. We met every night to pray for him. On the last evening he got up to sing as usual, and to the amazement of everyone, he sang like a bird. The audience burst into spontaneous applause because the man was clearly healed.

We are stunned when such things happen, but we shouldn't be. God has not changed since biblical times; He still loves His people, and He is still doing new things among His people. He is not merely a God of the past.

Outright skeptics point to the lack of *obvious* miracles as proof in their favor. Events labeled as "miracles" are actually just coincidence, they claim, or possibly scientific principles not yet discovered—just as to ancient cultures the existence of radio, television, telephones, or computers would seem miraculous.

In spite of widespread skepticism and doubt, I know that miracles happen today. We have reports of too many events that defy natural explanation. Some of the firmest believers in miracles are doctors who have witnessed inexplicable healings of terminal patients. Missionaries, too, and other reliable witnesses continue to report obvious miracles commonly occurring in Third World countries.

All this raises the question: Why doesn't God show His hand as clearly now as He did in biblical times? Why doesn't He make miracles so obvious they cannot be questioned?

One reason may simply be our own spiritual blindness. Living in the age of rationalism, we have lost a sense of the miraculous and therefore must fight all the harder to attune ourselves to God's work and voice. He acts and speaks a lot more than we realize. In John 12, we read of an incident in which a voice from heaven spoke audibly to Jesus. Some in the crowd heard it as the voice of an angel, whereas others heard it as merely a rumble of thunder. The closer you get to God, the more you will recognize miracles for what they are.

A second reason we don't see many obvious miracles may be that God wants us to have faith. Obvious miracles would almost compel belief and take from us the element of choice. Third, it seems to be a biblical principle that miracles flourish in an environment of belief. When people are more open to the supernatural, such as is common in today's Third World countries, miracles abound. Conversely, in cultures like ours that provide no fertile soil for belief to take root, widespread disbelief crowds out widespread miracles. The Bible tells us that even in Nazareth, Christ could do few miracles because of unbelief (Mark 6:5). So maybe we Westerners don't see more miracles because we don't really expect them to happen.

James tells us, "You do not have, because you do not ask God" (James 4:2 NIV). That's one reason we must never give up praying: because God's miracles often come in answer to believing prayer. God listens, and He can be persuaded.

We seem surprised that God can be compelled by our prayers. But the Bible shows it happening in several places. For example, He listened to Abraham's bargaining to save the city of Sodom. In another incident, God was so furious with the Israelites that He was poised to destroy them all and make Moses the sole inheritor of His promise. Moses pled with God to spare the people, and as a result we read, "So the Lord changed his mind about the terrible disaster he had threatened to bring on his people" (Exodus 32:14 NLT).

Many people tell me they have asked God for miracles, but the answer they wanted never came. I've had those experiences too, but I have learned that God does answer prayers; He just doesn't always give me the answer I want. He does, however, always give the answer that's best for me in the long run.

Maybe you need a miracle yourself, but you have little hope that God will step in and address your problem. I assure you, He can. It's happening all the time. I have seen impossible marriages put back together, parents and estranged children reconciled, chronic or even fatal diseases healed, and numerous other miracles where God stepped in and did the impossible. And He can do it for you.

I was speaking in Hawaii, and at the altar call an elderly lady rolled herself down the aisle in a wheelchair. She was ninety-five years old, and this was the first time she had ever been in a Christian church. That night she asked Jesus to be her Savior, and she was so joyful that she continually repeated, "Isn't God good to let me live long enough to come to Him?"

That lady's conversion was a miracle. In fact, it's always a miracle when one comes to Christ, because salvation itself—with the God of heaven coming down to suffer, die, and be raised from the dead for human sin—is a miracle of cosmic proportions.

Maybe you think, *God cannot possibly save me. You don't know what I've done.* Well, the good news is that God is still in the miracle business. He's always doing a new thing, and He can do it for you, just as He did for me.

I am living proof that God still works miracles. The very fact that I am here and able to communicate today is the result of God moving to shape the events of that cold, January morning in 1989. I mentioned these events in the first week's lessons, but this week I want to consider them from one specific angle—the miraculous.

The First Miracle. The EMTs who arrived at the accident scene found no pulse or heartbeat and declared that I had died on impact at 11:45 a.m. The pastor who prayed over my body recognized signs of life in me at 1:15 p.m.—a lapsed time of ninety minutes. To be dead for ninety minutes, with no heartbeat and no blood circulating to keep limbs and organs alive, is medically irrevocable.

The Second Miracle. Pastor Dick Onerecker left the conference before I did but stopped for a coffee warm-up. That stop put him behind me, allowing him to arrive at the scene and pray for me.

The Third Miracle. The EMTs could not legally remove my body from the accident scene until a county coroner arrived to officially pronounce me dead. But the coronor was not available. Had he been available, I would have been taken immediately to a morgue, and my death would have been permanent.

The Fourth Miracle. Dick arrived on the scene wanting to pray for the injured. Though I was dead, and Dick did not believe in praying for the dead, he felt a strong impulse from God to pray for me anyway—and so he did.

The Fifth Miracle. Dick crawled into the smashed car to pray over my body. After a time, and to his great shock, the body returned to life.

The Sixth Miracle. The EMTs told Dick that I had massive internal and head injuries. He prayed that I would be delivered from those injuries. When I arrived at the Houston hospital, doctors found no injuries to my head or internal organs.

The Seventh Miracle. The EMTs called my wife to inform her of the accident, omitting the detail that I was dead. She immediately sent out word to churches, asking for widespread prayers. Thousands of Christians prayed for me. Although my survival seemed impossible, God answered those prayers.

Making Sense of the Miraculous

The Bible shows a definite connection between prayers and miracles.

Moses called on the Lord to provide water for the Israelites, and water gushed from a rock (Exodus 17). In the contest with the priests of Baal in 1 Kings 18, Elijah prayed for fire to light his altar, and the flame came down immediately. In Acts 12 we read of an angel releasing Peter from prison after Christians had gathered to pray.

Certainly, every prayer God answers involves a divine intervention in our lives, and thus is a miracle. Yet I know that good, dedicated, Spirit-led Christians have many beliefs and opinions about miracles. Just what is a miracle? What distinguishes a miracle from other supernatural activities? And what does it mean when miracles don't happen in response to our prayers?

To answer the first question, a simple definition that works for me is that a miracle occurs when God intervenes in the natural course of events to produce His own desired results. Some people distinguish God's miracles from His providence. The term *providence* usually means God bringing about His desired result through natural means instead of manipulating the laws of nature. When God works providentially, the result seems so natural that we are often blind to the fact He works at all—like the man who fell from a cliff and cried out, "God, please save me!" At that moment his fall was arrested and he found himself hanging in midair. "Never mind, God," he said. "My pants just caught on a tree limb." In trying to distinguish God's miracles from His providence, I side with C. S. Lewis, who believed that God works both ways but who saw no essential difference between the two.

What separates the miracles of Christianity from those claimed by other religions? For one, when a *real* miracle occurs, it's always God at work. Biblical miracle workers never relied on their own power; they acted as agents for the power of God. Even Jesus did not use His own innate power to work miracles while in human form on earth. He allowed the power of God the Father to work through Him (see John 5:19). The miracles of Christianity are never arbitrary, vindictive, or destructive of good as God created it either. And godly miracles do not violate creation. Thus, you never find biblical apostles or prophets turning a man into a toad or causing snakes to sprout from a person's head. Instead, God's miracles restore creation, as in healings and raisings from the dead, or they demonstrate God's control of it. His miracles sometimes speed up a natural process—for example, turning water to wine instantly instead of allowing nature to do it slowly. And some miracles undo the effects of fallen nature, as when Jesus calmed a storm.

However, even among those who are open to the possibility of divine miracles today, there is one barrier to belief that most Christians wrestle with at one time or another: the dilemma of seemingly unanswered prayers. Many become disillusioned when they don't get the response they prayed for. At these times it's easy to lose one's sense of what answered prayer means. I struggled with this too during my long recovery, begging the Lord to just let me die and return to the ecstasies of heaven.

Obviously, I'm still here. Still waiting. Yet I firmly believe God always answers our prayers; He just doesn't always answer as we hoped.

Why not? First, we read in James 4:3 that some prayers are simply not proper prayers. They are self-centered demands—essentially, "I want what I want when I want it" requests. Usually in these cases, God simply answers no.

Second, sometimes we unwittingly pray for logical impossibilities. The farmer who just planted his crop prays for rain, while the homeowner across the fence with a leaky roof prays for a dry spell. It's impossible for both prayers to be granted simultaneously. As I look back, I can see how my prayers for death contradicted the prayers of Dick Onerecker and thousands of Christians who'd prayed for me to live. Only one of us was going to get a "yes."

The third reason some prayers are not granted is that what we sometimes pray is not in the will of God. In my situation, God had a plan for me that involved experiencing heaven and enduring suffering. My prayer for death worked against that plan, so He had to tell me no. This is also why God did not grant Christ's prayer in Gethsemane. The plan engraved on the foundations of the world was that Jesus would be sacrificed for our sins. Removing the cup of suffering from Him would have undone our redemption.

Fourth, God sometimes denies our prayers in order to give us something better. That's exactly what He did in response to Christ's prayer for deliverance from crucifixion. We read that immediately after Jesus' prayer, " . . . an angel from heaven appeared and strengthened him" (Luke 22:43 NLT). Christ didn't avoid torture and death, but He received strength to bear it and accomplish the salvation of the world.

The bottom line is, if we want our prayers to be effective, and we long to see miracles occur, we need to pray specifically, believing God will answer. He has promised that He will. We should also pray regularly. In fact, Paul tells us to pray all the time (1 Thessalonians 5:17). This doesn't mean spending twenty-four hours a day on your knees. It means developing the habit of prayer and including God as your constant companion.

When the Bible tells us that Abraham and Moses walked and talked with God, it is describing men who loved God so much that they engaged Him in continual conversation. God longs for this kind of intimacy with each one of us. It's what He intended at the beginning of creation, when He walked with Adam and Eve in the cool of the day. And it's what He intends for us today.

1. Do you know someone who has experienced a miracle? Share their story.

2. How often do you pray for "impossible" things? Is it easier to ask for God's intervention in a crisis or in the everyday? Why?

3. To what degree do you believe the promise of Matthew 21:22? How do we typically explain away unanswered prayers?

4. Contrast Christ's words in Matthew 21:21–22 with the events in 2 Samuel 12:13–16, 19–23. Discuss the meaning of these two outcomes. What role does prayer have in the miraculous?

5. How did God answer Paul's prayer in 2 Corinthians 12:7–9a (NLT)? How did Paul respond (verses 9b–10)?

LIVE WHAT YOU'VE LEARNED

Jesus Himself said, "Ask, and it will be given to you; seek, and you will find; knock, and it will be opened to you" (Matthew 7:7 NKJV). There are times when the only reason something is impossible is because we don't think to ask the Lord to work in our situation. This week, watch for miracles, whether they be great or small. Invite God to participate in every aspect of your day by asking, seeking, and knocking upon the doors of heaven.

WEEK 2

DAY 1

WHAT IS
A MIRACLE?

"Then he told John's disciples, 'Go back to John and tell him what you have seen and heard—the blind see, the lame walk, the lepers are cured, the deaf hear, the dead are raised to life, and the Good News is being preached to the poor.'"
— Luke 7:22 (NLT)

Some scientists are now saying that the conditions for life to have occurred on this planet required so much fine-tuning that the odds of it happening by chance are astronomical. So astronomical as to be rationally impossible. The earth had to be a certain distance from the sun. The sun had to be a certain temperature. Gravity had to be a certain strength . . . The slightest variation in any of the millions of minute factors necessary for sustaining life would have prevented life altogether.

The events surrounding my accident were much like that. Any little change in circumstances would have blown the entire picture, and I would not have survived. If the county coroner had been available, I would have been whisked off to the morgue. If Dick Onerecker's wife had not needed a coffee warm-up, he would not have been at the accident scene to pray for me. If he had not prayed for healing of internal injuries, I might be a vegetable today even if I had survived. For these and other events to come together just as they did, and in the right sequence, meant some hand outside nature had to be involved.

Whether God's hand is visible and spectacular or invisible and quiet, it's still Him doing the work. When God's hand works for our benefit, it shows that nature is under His control and that He can bend it to His will. I call that a miracle.

1. What are some of the terms we use to describe "every-day miracles"?

2. Share about a time when, in hindsight, you're sure God's hand was at work in your life.

3. Compare John 2:11–13 with John 20:30–31. In what way did Jesus' earthly miracles remain unchanged from beginning to end?

4. What lesson can you take from the promise and the prayer found in Mark 9:20b–24?

Miracles are a retelling in small letters of the very same story which is written across the whole world in letters too large for some of us to see.

—

C. S. Lewis

5. Describe the relationship between evidence and faith according to Hebrews 11:1.

Father, I fear I have often failed to recognize Your hand. May You never cease to intervene in ways that accomplish Your will for my life.

WEEK 2

DAY 2

HAS THE AGE OF MIRACLES CEASED?

"I tell you the truth, anyone who believes in me will do the same works I have done, and even greater works."
— John 14:12a (NLT)

Many people are skeptical of my death experience and my attribution of miracles to the events surrounding it. Their possible explanations for my experience in heaven range from psychological hallucination to a dream composed of what I've read in the Bible. Some skeptics think the events that worked in sequence to save my life are merely an extraordinary set of fortunate coincidences. Some Christians have trouble believing because various elements in my story violate their theology. For others, my experience contradicts their embedded concept of heaven. And I find that a large number of Christians believe miracles simply do not happen today.

I don't try to defend or explain my experience. I know what happened to me, and I know it was real. I witnessed too many things I could never have imagined, things for which I had no existing data in my mind. In addition, I recognize the difference between a dream and concrete reality. What I experienced still dominates my being, and it has turned my life upside down, completely altering my outlook and giving me a new perspective on reality. Most importantly, my experience has been meaningful to many others, giving them hope, assurance, and the faith and fortitude to carry on in the face of suffering.

God still works miracles because we still have needs. And He often does His work in wholly unexpected ways. Aren't you glad He is willing to reach down into nature and massage events for our benefit? It's all because of His great love. His miracles will never cease because His love will never cease (Ephesians 3:17–19).

1. What do Isaiah 55:8–9 and Romans 11:33–34 say about our ability to figure out God? Does this comfort you or worry you?

2. What does David express in Psalm 27:13? Do you share his confidence?

3. Read 2 Corinthians 5:7. In what ways are we blind? What challenges does this present?

4. Read Paul's declaration in 2 Timothy 1:12, then write a similar statement of faith in your own words.

A coincidence is

a small miracle

in which God

chooses to remain

anonymous.

—

Anonymous

Father, I'm grateful that while You set the laws of nature on their courses, You are attentive to my needs. Please open the eyes of my faith to Your miraculous activity.

29

DAY 3

PRAYER AND MIRACLES

"Then Jesus told them, 'I tell you the truth, if you have faith and don't doubt, you can . . . even say to this mountain, "May you be lifted up and thrown into the sea," and it will happen."
— Matthew 21:21 (NLT)

My accident motivated people to ask for some pretty outrageous things. The EMTs on the scene told Dick Onerecker that massive internal injuries had caused my death. Undeterred, Dick wormed his way through the back of the flattened wreckage and prayed. One of his requests was that my internal injuries would be healed.

Upon being informed of the accident, my wife instantly called our church and other Christians, who in turn called others until thousands were praying for my survival, not knowing I was already dead. Later, when I was in the hospital and it was doubtful whether my arm and leg could be saved, a chain of prayers was activated yet again.

Every one of these prayers unambiguously called for miracles. Every one was answered, some of them spectacularly. I returned to life, with no internal damage, and it didn't cost me an arm and a leg.

When you think about it, every petitionary prayer is a request for a miracle; we are asking God to effect a change in the course of natural events. Whether or not God responds as we've asked, our prayers are never pointless. They increase our connection with God and our awareness of Him. Prayer also gives us insight into God's will so that we can align our minds with His.

When we become so intimate with God that our will and His are one, answers to our prayers will become more frequent, more obvious, and more spectacular. In a word, they will be more miraculous. And we will be changed people.

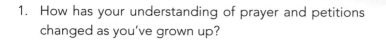

1. How has your understanding of prayer and petitions changed as you've grown up?

2. Read Matthew 7:7–11. What "good things" do you long to ask your heavenly Father but haven't? Why have you hesitated?

The most wonderful thing about miracles is that they sometimes happen.

—

G. K. Chesterton

3. What three things does the Lord do, according to Psalm 10:17? How do these actions influence our prayer life?

4. Look at the Lord's Prayer in Matthew 6:9–13. What things did Jesus pray about? Does their importance vary?

Father, teach me to pray in Your will, and then strengthen my faith so that I will fearlessly pray bold prayers, asking You for bold answers.

WEEK 2

DAY **4**

CAN GOD BE COMPELLED?

"So I say to you: Ask and it will be given to you; seek and you will find; knock and the door will be opened to you."
— Luke 11:9 (NIV)

Early in my recovery from the accident I developed pneumonia because, with my crushed arm and leg in traction, I couldn't sit up for the breathing treatments. The doctors said the solution was to amputate those limbs so that I could be freed from the traction devices. Instead, my wife again initiated widespread prayers from Christians everywhere, and the next morning my pneumonia was gone.

Without those prayers, I would now be a double amputee. Had nature taken its normal course, I'd be a severely crippled man now. The prayers of Christians compelled God to interfere with nature and save my arm, my leg, and my life.

Do you wonder why the Lord of the universe listens to us lowly humans and allows us to influence His decisions? The answer is that He has made us participants in accomplishing His will on earth. We were created to be God's agents—subrulers under Him, with dominion over animals and vegetation.

Even though for now, Satan has usurped our place as lords of the earth, God still looks to us to fulfill the role for which we were created. If we accept this task responsibly, He supplies the power to accomplish it. And if we get on God's wavelength and pray responsibly, He listens to our ideas and requests just as a father listens to those of his children. Then He lets us experience the result of our prayers.

God wants us to learn all this now, because as Jesus' parable of the talents indicates (Matthew 25), it is a foreshadowing of what we will do in heaven.

1. Share about a time when you wanted something so badly that you were blinded to the potential consequences.

2. Read Psalm 34:15, John 14:13–14, and Hebrews 4:16. Do these verses incline you to petition God with greater care? With greater frequency? Explain.

3. What rule of thumb can be found in Matthew 6:33 and 1 John 5:14? Does this limit what we can pray about?

4. What does Matthew 18:18–19 say God will do if you responsibly represent Him in the world? In light of that, what should you be willing to do for Him?

[Miracles are]

the extraordinary

work of God

that involves His

immediate and

unmistakable

intervention in

the physical realm

in a way that

contravenes natural

processes.

—

Phil Johnson

Lord, help me not to hesitate in taking on any task You place before me.

33

DAY 5

DOES GOD ANSWER EVERY PRAYER?

"When you ask, you do not receive, because you ask with wrong motives, that you may spend what you get on your pleasures." — James 4:3 (NIV)

As I lay confined in that hospital bed with no guarantee that I would recover, time passed at the pace of an oak tree growing. It became clear that even if I did recover, I would lead a diminished life of continuing pain and limited mobility. To make matters worse, my tantalizing taste of heaven made my present life all the more intolerable. I can't count the times I pled with God to relieve me of my misery and return me to the bliss of heaven.

That prayer was not answered in the way I'd hoped, and I couldn't understand why. God had affirmatively responded to the prayers of Dick Onerecker and the church when they prayed for my life. Why not mine?

Today, with the benefit of hindsight, I can see that God did indeed answer my prayer for deliverance: by giving me something better than I prayed for. He gave me new insights into the nature of heaven, deeper empathy for those in pain, and greater patience amid difficulties. These gifts became the foundation of my ministry, which has benefited thousands who needed hope and endurance.

When wrestling with the workings of prayer, it's important to remember that although God knows our needs before we ask (Matthew 6:8), He wants us to ask because we need to learn to align our will with His. Prayer is our communication line with God. We learn to listen to Him as He listens to us. Part of the listening is observing which prayers are answered yes and which are answered no—and allowing Him to shape our hearts through each one.

1. What reassurance do Proverbs 16:9 and 19:21 offer in the face of yet-to-be-answered prayers?

2. Can you echo the prophet's words in Micah 7:7? What goes through your mind between the asking and the answers?

3. What's the simplest way to deal with the hindrances to prayer mentioned in Isaiah 59:2 and James 4:3?

4. Look up Ephesians 3:20. Why is it encouraging to know this about the Lord?

5. Read and summarize Hebrews 10:32–39. Then memorize the command in verse 35 and live accordingly!

O believing brethren! What an instrument is this which God hath put into your hands! Prayer moves Him that moves the universe.

—

Robert Murray McCheyne

Lord, thank You for all your answered prayers—not just the yeses.

WHO WILL WE SEE IN HEAVEN?

"These things I have written to you who believe in the name of the Son of God, that you may know that you have eternal life, and that you may continue to believe in the name of the Son of God." — 1 John 5:13 (NKJV)

The People I Saw in Heaven

When I arrived in heaven after my accident, the first person to greet me was my grandfather. "Welcome home, Donnie!" he bellowed, grinning from ear to ear. I was ecstatic to see this man because he had been the single most positive influence in my life. Grandfather Kulbeth had been a carpenter, and his hands and face had borne many of the scars of his trade. But now his scars were gone. He was perfect in every way, yet he was still clearly identifiable as my grandfather.

With my grandfather was a stunning array of people—other relatives, friends, neighbors, a couple of my teachers, and many others whose deaths had preceded mine. It wasn't long before I realized why these particular people formed my greeting committee: Each of them had played some part in helping me get to heaven. Each was a dedicated Christian with a real heart for the Lord.

I believe the makeup of my greeters goes a long way toward

telling us who we will see in heaven: everyone who makes the decision to give his or her heart to Christ.

The Bible tells us plainly that He is the only way to heaven. Only He died for us. Only He became a man so He could bear our sin and take it to the cross. Only He is the accepted sacrifice for the sins that separate us from God. Only He was resurrected to blaze the trail to a new life freed from the curse of death.

That message is not politically correct in our culture of extreme tolerance and postmodern ambiguity. Amid such feel-good individualism, truth is "whatever works for me," which means two things: a person must not claim any truth to be truly true, and one must accept every truth-claim as being as valid as any other. Yet in spite of popular views, all religions are not the same. Eastern religions such as Buddhism and Hinduism believe in an altogether different kind of afterlife than Christianity. Their adherents do not expect to find joy or to have resurrected bodies; they expect to be absorbed into some vague, cosmic consciousness that obliterates all traces of individual personality.

Clearly, their road will not lead to God's heaven.

Sometimes we're told that to believe something sincerely makes it true. But we know better in our daily lives. To believe sincerely that a rat poison pellet is your blood pressure medicine will not keep you from suffering the consequences of your mistake. So why do we abandon such common sense when it comes to religion? The tragedy of such distorted thinking will be realized when people spend their lives on their own road, only to find that they have reached someplace other than their intended destination.

The Bible tells us that our sins will keep us from God's presence; without the shedding of Christ's blood, there is no remedy for sin. Period. End of story. Critics of Christianity proclaim that this is unfair because so many people have never heard of Christ. Why would God condemn them, they ask.

Paul responds by telling us that God's grace will cover people who are unaware of Christ but who follow the dictates of righteousness God has written on the heart of every human (Romans 2:14–16). But even then, the fact remains that salvation is extended to those people by the grace of God and the blood of Christ. There is no other path to God.

One question people often ask is whether people in heaven know what's going on here on earth. I certainly didn't during my ninety minutes in heaven. In fact, I had no thoughts whatsoever of my loved ones on earth, even though I adore my wife and sons. So when a grieving mother who had lost her three-year-old daughter wanted to know if her little girl missed her, I had to gently respond, "No, in heaven there is no pain, no tears, and no suffering. The people in heaven have no awareness of separation from those on earth." But as I pointed out, if we truly love those who have gone on before us, would we want them to experience our grief or know our pain? Surely not.

Those in heaven know who is there, but they do not know who is absent, and thus they experience no anguish over separations. However, they will know when their loved ones arrive and will meet them joyfully, just as my friends and family members met me.

Heaven's citizens are experiencing nothing but utter joy and elation at all times. Though we can't completely understand it, the sorrows of earth have been filtered out. I am convinced that this is a permanent condition in heaven. In fact, when you think about it, it's a necessary condition in order for heaven to be heaven. If we carried in our memory any thought that brought sorrow or anxiety, it would obstruct our happiness. Instead of being a place where all tears are wiped away, heaven would be merely an extension of our troubled life on earth.

The obvious question, then, is, how can we bear to not think about the people we loved so much on earth? Isn't it selfish to no longer be concerned about whether you are with them? Whether they grieve for you? Whether they will make it to heaven themselves?

I cannot overstress what we Christians seem to have trouble realizing: death separates loved ones only temporarily.

When I conducted the funeral of my sister-in-law, who died at age thirty-nine, I said, "This is a great loss, and we grieve because the separation is real and painful. But the good news is that it won't last. When you know where someone is, they are not really lost, and we can find comfort in the assurance that we will see her again."

Those who persevere in the Christian walk on earth will join those already in heaven. Time doesn't exist in eternity, so heaven's inhabitants don't "lose" time, and therefore they don't experience the separation that we do on earth. One joy completely fills their being, making them unaware of all others. They do not miss what they are not aware of.

Maybe we can clarify the concept by comparing it to a common experience on earth. If you have children, no doubt you love them with all your heart. But when you are embracing your spouse, you do not think about your children. Does this mean you don't love them? No, it simply means that there are moments when your mind is so full of one love that other loves are crowded out. That's how it is in heaven.

Because of these truths, it is not a cruelty that loved ones in heaven are not aware of us on earth. Grief and separation are meaningless for them. And that makes heaven an even greater reward and joy!

The absence of separation sorrow in heaven is apparently not the case in hell. In Luke 16 Christ tells the parable of Lazarus and the rich man. Lazarus went to heaven and the rich man to hell, where he remembered everything from his past. He knew the wickedness of his brothers, he knew Lazarus was in heaven, and this knowledge caused him terrible agony. To know that he had missed out forever on the greatest joy a person could ever experience was certainly a significant factor in his torment.

On the other hand, the parable says nothing of Lazarus's awareness. My own experience convinces me that he had no knowledge of being separated from the people he left behind, whether godly or not. He was (and still is!) simply experiencing eternal bliss in the only place where sorrow and grief are banished forever.

Another question I'm often asked is, why was my loved one taken while I was left here to grieve? The answer I can give is that there is a reason for you to be here. If you don't know that reason, it may be that you simply haven't asked. You are still here because God has something yet for you to do. Ask Him with a surrendered heart, and you will come to know what that reason is.

I'm certain it will entail serving others somehow. In Matthew 25:31–46 Christ shows us the importance of this. Whether we love God and have faith in Him is demonstrated by how we love others and minister to their needs. We are to feed the hungry, clothe the naked, visit the sick, and be hospitable to strangers. In other words, assist the family in the stalled car; the father who can't meet the house payment because of a job loss; the frazzled single mother worn down with work, tending kids, and paying bills; and the recent widow suddenly living alone. Christ promises that people who love deeply enough to do such deeds in His name will inherit eternal life.

How Heaven Changed My Thinking about Death

There's no question about it: death is a terrible thing. It is such an insidious horror that God has gone to enormous, cosmic lengths to assure its defeat. Until that victory is complete, however, we still have to traverse the dark valley of death. Yet thanks to Christ's sacrifice and His subsequent resurrection, we who are in Him can look at death in an altogether different way. No longer is it the ultimate tragedy.

Yes, death still hurts us. We grieve when we lose loved ones. But as Paul said, we need not grieve like those who have no hope of resurrection (1 Thessalonians 4:13). For Christians, resurrection and reunion with loved ones is assured.

At death, we will also experience reunion with God, who has loved us more dearly than all the people we've ever known. At death, we will leave behind all the problems we face in this messed-up world. No more snags or failures in our work. No more difficulties with relationships. No more natural disasters, diseases, rust, rot, decay, pain, fear, loss, crime, deceit, envy, or hardship. Thanks to Christ, death—fearsome and dark as it is—has become the passageway out of the bad and the ugly and into the good and the beautiful.

Yet in my travels and speaking, I find that many Christians do not look at death in this way. Unlike Paul, they see death as the ultimate tragedy, the ruin of happiness, the blight that snuffs out the light in their soul. While most Christians believe intellectually that they will see their lost loved one again, the loss often plunges their hearts into a lasting gloom, as if the separation were permanent.

I fear that many Christians have come to think much like the world around us, which puts so much emphasis on creating a heaven here and now that we come perilously close to writing off the true heaven God is preparing for us. What does it matter whether we die at age eight or age eighty? The longest life on earth is a mere wisp of a vapor in comparison to eternity.

I don't mean for that statement to sound callous; I fully recognize that grief is real and painful. I've felt it. But I've also experienced heaven, which has shown me the true perspective from which to see life and death. I saw people who had died, and they were deliriously happy, in superb physical health, and had not an ounce of pain, grief, or sorrow. Isn't that how you long to be?

That is how you can be. That is how your loved ones in heaven exist now. I assure you, you will live a happier, more contented, more joyful life now if you can adjust your perspective to see the temporary separation of death in this light.

Lastly, one of the most persistent questions I get about heaven is whether or not animals will be there. Pet owners in particular naturally want to know if Fido or Fluffy will join them. Though I didn't get a look inside the gates of heaven, I believe animals will be there. I'll give you four reasons:

First, we have scriptures that seem to indicate their presence. Isaiah 11:6–9 speaks of a number of animals living harmoniously in the New Earth. Revelation depicts the conquering Jesus riding out of heaven on a horse. In Revelation 19:11–14 He is joined by the angelic host who also ride out on horses.

Second, redemption includes not only humans but the whole of creation. When man fell, he pulled all creation into corruption with him, and all creation will be redeemed with man. Redemption means restoration of God's creation ideal. John Wesley believed *everything* must include animals. He said, "The whole brute creation will then, undoubtedly, be restored . . . to the vigor, strength, and swiftness which they had at their creation."

Third, at the end of His six days of creation, God declared all creation good. Creation included the animals, and it's not likely that God would allow Satan to forever ruin anything that He pronounced as good.

Fourth, throughout the Bible animals are depicted as being integral participants in the human story. Ravens feed Elijah. A fish swallows Jonah. Balaam's donkey talks. Lambs are temple sacrifices. Working animals are allowed a Sabbath rest along with humans. Jesus rides a donkey into Jerusalem. If animals are part of what makes life complete for us now, it's likely they will remain with us when creation is redeemed.

The greater question, though, is: *Who* will we see in heaven? The biblical answer is clear: Those who know Christ as Lord and Savior and submit their hearts to Him.

Are you going? I am. I've been there, and I can't wait to go back. And when I do, I want to see you there at the gate with me.

1. Are you confident that you will be in heaven? Why or why not?

2. Who do you expect to reunite with in heaven? What role did they play in your life? When the time comes, whose welcoming committee do you expect to be on?

3. What part of heaven are you most looking forward to?

4. Read 2 Corinthians 4:16–18. How does heaven compare to everything else we know? What hints are Christians given about how to view death?

5. According to 2 Peter 1:5–10, what should those who will "receive a rich welcome into the eternal kingdom of our Lord" (v. 11 NIV) be doing right now to prepare?

LIVE WHAT YOU'VE LEARNED

Who are you eager to speak with when you reach your eternal home? Think about all the people you know who you expect to reunite with in heaven. Next, consider the various people you know of—but haven't met personally—whose testimonies, lives, ministries, books, songs, and efforts have contributed to your spiritual growth. Then, reflect on those lives you know well because their stories are found in the pages of Scripture. What do you want to say to them or ask them about? Reflect on this today.

WEEK 3

DAY 1

WILL WE HAVE REAL BODIES IN HEAVEN?

"[W]hen the trumpet sounds, . . . we who are living will also be transformed. For our dying bodies must be transformed into bodies that will never die. " — 1 Corinthians 15:52–53 (NLT)

Before I was in ministry, I was a television news anchor. One night after finishing the ten o'clock news, I had just arrived home when my mother called. "Papa is dying!" she cried. Though we administered CPR and got him on an ambulance, my grandfather died on the way to the hospital. I was heartbroken at his loss.

This grandfather was the first person I saw in heaven. In fact, seeing him was how I knew I was in heaven. Though he was clearly recognizable, the man standing before me was nothing like the dying old man I had seen in that ambulance. He was now robust and filled with joy. And when he hugged me, it was a strong, solid, energetic embrace. Not wispy or ghostlike in any way.

The same was true of the other loved ones I saw in heaven. Every one of them was hearty and healthy, with all the genetic flaws caused by the contamination of the Fall corrected to perfection. Their facial features and bodies were stunningly beautiful, though their ages were hard to discern. Simply put, they were all exactly the ages they should be in order to be their ideal selves.

The entire experience gave me a tantalizing glimpse of what our resurrected bodies will be like. And it confirms both what Paul told us about the body in 1 Corinthians 15 and the kind of body Christ had after His resurrection. Every person I saw was a testimony to the fact that we will someday be what God originally intended us to be in the beginning of creation.

1. What kinds of things do you look forward to? How does that anticipation affect your wait?

2. What transformation can God's people expect, according to Philippians 3:21 and 1 John 3:2?

If you have a dear one in Heaven your heart yearns to see, do not despair. . . . Your beloved one is only "lost awhile."

—

Herbert Lockyer

3. Assuming we will someday have new bodies formed by the hand of God (see 2 Corinthians 5:1), what do you expect your new body to be like?

4. What awaits us in 1 Peter 1:3–4? How is our plain old, everyday hope transformed?

Father, I thank You for Christ's resurrection and its inherent promise of transformation. Help me to see everyone I encounter today in the light of the perfection You intend.

DAY 2

WHAT GETS US INTO HEAVEN?

"[S]o that as sin reigned in death, even so grace might reign through righteousness to eternal life through Jesus Christ our Lord." — Romans 5:21 (NKJV)

In heaven, I was filled with indescribable joy at seeing and hugging all those people I had loved—people who'd had some part in my spiritual journey. Besides my grandfather, our neighbor Mrs. Norris was there. She would come by on Sunday mornings to pick up us neighborhood kids and take us to church. I was also greeted by two teachers who had loved me and often talked to me about Christ.

Then there was Mike Wood. Mike was my best friend growing up, and he was the most devoted young Christian I ever knew. He persistently invited me to Sunday school until I gave in and started going. He was a popular kid who lettered four years in high school football, basketball, and track, but he was a hero to me because of the way he lived the Christian life. Upon graduation, he received a full scholarship to LSU, but he was killed in a car wreck at age nineteen.

These were only a few of the many who joyously greeted me. The roles they played in my life varied. Some of the help they gave me was obvious: one took me to church; another told me about Jesus. Others encouraged me or simply lived the Christian life before me. Perhaps some didn't even know they were helping me at all. But every one of them lived their lives under God and reflected His nature in some way.

Even when we are not called to perform overt or dramatic deeds for others, it is vitally important that we live every moment with our hearts submitted to God, faithfully reflecting Him. Someone may be watching who will be eternally affected by our behavior.

1. Have you ever discovered that some action of yours influenced another person (for good or for worse)? How did that make you feel?

2. What are we to do with the grace that abounds toward us, according to 2 Corinthians 9:8?

3. Read Galatians 6:8. What are you planting right now? What is the harvest you can expect?

4. How are we urged to live in Colossians 1:10 (NKJV)? What effects do good works have in our lives?

No two Christians

will ever meet for

the last time.

—

Anonymous

Lord, please grant me a loving heart that reflects Your heart and shows others the way to You.

DAY 3

WILL THERE BE ANIMALS IN HEAVEN?

"In that day the wolf and the lamb will live together; the leopard will lie down with the baby goat. The calf and the yearling will be safe with the lion, and a little child will lead them all." — Isaiah 11:6 (NLT)

A pet owner once told me, "If my Fluffy can't be in heaven with me, then I don't want to go."

As an animal lover myself, I would be glad to have animals in heaven. Especially if they're like Old Yeller, the dog from the classic Disney movie. He's a stray who wanders onto the farm of an American frontier family and gets into all kinds of entertaining mishaps. At the climax of the story, the younger son is threatened by a bear—and Old Yeller ultimately sacrifices his life to save the boy's life.

Such movies reinforce our thinking that "good" animals, at least, should be allowed in heaven. I saw no animals in my brief time there, but I did not get inside the gate either. The fact that I didn't see animals in heaven doesn't mean they're not there; in fact, I believe they will be there, given what I read in the Bible. Though when that woman told me she wouldn't be happy in heaven without Fluffy, I did shudder internally. Did she love her pet more than God? The Bible has a word for loving anything more than God: *idolatry*. If we choose anything above God, Matthew 10:37 tells us that He is likely to honor that choice by allowing us to remain outside of heaven.

Whether animals will be in heaven is an interesting question worthy of discussion, but the fundamental question is, will you be in heaven? That is something you can determine by choosing to love God more than your pet.

1. How do you feel at the thought that animals may be in heaven? Explain why.

2. Why might God want animals in heaven?

3. Read Isaiah 65:17, then the renewal of this promise in 2 Peter 3:13. What might remain the same? What do you think will be changed?

4. In the following passages, what do these "now" and "then" differences tell us about the effects of the Fall? About life in heaven?

   Numbers 23:24 & Isaiah 65:25

   Jeremiah 5:6 & Isaiah 11:6

   John 10:12 & Isaiah 11:6

God will prepare

everything for

our perfect

happiness in

heaven, and if it

takes my dog being

there, I believe

he'll be there.

—

Billy Graham

Father, thank You for animals and the many ways they enrich our lives.

WEEK 3

4

WILL ALL RELIGIONS GET TO HEAVEN?

"There is salvation in no one else! God has given no other name under heaven by which we must be saved."
— Acts 4:12 (NLT)

If you ask your travel agent, "Which plane should I take to Chicago?" and she replies, "It really doesn't matter because they all arrive at the same place," you know she's spouting nonsense.

If two college students on their way back to their Houston campus accidentally turn onto an intersecting road that's headed straight for Indianapolis, they can stay on that road for as long as they want, but it will never get them to Houston.

Though in everyday life we know the wrong plane or the wrong road will never get us to the right destination, a growing number of people today believe you can reach heaven by virtually any spiritual route. But the Bible tells us, "How shall we escape if we ignore such a great salvation?" (Hebrews 2:3 NIV).

Since we are aware of the route God has provided in His Son Jesus, we need to follow it. Some people allow themselves to be deterred because no one is sure what God will do with those who never hear the salvation message. It is God's business to deal with them, and we are assured that He is always just and merciful. Whatever provision God has made for others gives us no excuse for neglecting the salvation that is offered to us.

As Narnia's Lion-God Aslan sometimes told those who asked about the fate of others, "I tell no one any story but his own." Our task is to write our own story, or as Paul said, "Continue to work out your salvation with fear and trembling" (Philippians 2:12 NIV). We have been shown the right road; it's up to us to travel it.

1. Do you have friends—Christian or not—who use a "smorgasbord" approach to faith? What happens when we pick and choose which parts of the Bible to believe?

2. How does Proverbs 16:25 answer the cultural tendency toward individualized religion?

3. Have you heard people try to explain away Jesus' words in John 14:6? How?

4. Given what Acts 4:12 says about Jesus, why do you think so many people search for a Plan B?

No man may go to heaven who hath not sent his heart thither before.

—

Anonymous

Lord, I'm forever grateful for Your willingness to provide us a path to heaven. Show me how to guide others who question Your fairness or are seeking alternatives.

WEEK 3

WILL WE MISS OUR LOVED ONES?

"He will wipe every tear from their eyes. There will be no more death or mourning or crying or pain, for the old order of things has passed away." — Revelation 21:4 (NIV)

When I was in heaven I had no awareness of anything but the present moment. My joyful reunion with people I had loved on earth and the wonders and delights of heaven completely dominated my senses. So much so that I didn't once think of my beloved wife and kids during my time in heaven. I didn't grieve over the fact that I was separated from them, and I felt no concern about the grief they were feeling back on earth.

I realize how callous that sounds. In fact, when I shared that piece of my experience with my father-in-law, it angered him. But later he came to understand that it didn't signal a lack of love for his daughter; it is simply the inevitable condition of everyone who lives in heaven. The love and delights they experience there totally absorb every fiber of their being. Their minds and hearts are so full of love and joy that everything but the present moment is crowded out by waves upon waves of continual ecstasy, with no space for even one wisp of sorrow to intrude.

Thankfully, these unique aspects of heaven will not hinder your ultimate reunion with loved ones in any way. Though thoughts of you don't enter their mind while you are separated, they are thankfully feeling nothing now but total happiness. And you can be certain they will be filled with love and joy for you when you arrive in heaven.

For all our loved ones who are there, the sorrows of earth have been filtered out and they are experiencing only the purest joy and elation. Really, would we want anything less for them?

1. Recall your deepest moments of happiness. Now try to imagine how heaven will exceed them.

2. Reflect on Revelation 22:3–5. Are you looking forward to meeting Jesus? Are you nervous? Explain your feelings.

Earth has no

sorrow that heaven

cannot heal.

—

Sir Thomas More

3. How does Jesus describe our present grief and our future joy in John 16:20–22?

4. Though we can't begin to fathom all that God has prepared for His own (1 Corinthians 2:9), what glimpses do Psalm 16:11, Isaiah 60:19, and Revelation 7:16–17 offer?

Father, I praise You that those I love who are already in heaven are experiencing a joy that no sorrow on earth can touch.

WHAT IS HEAVEN LIKE?

"No eye has seen, no ear has heard, and no mind has imagined what God has prepared for those who love him." — 1 Corinthians 2:9 (NLT)

What I Saw in Heaven

I am about to attempt the impossible: I will try to tell you as well as I can the physical attributes of heaven as I saw them. Human language can't convey the grandeur, the magnificence, the vividness, and the sense of absolute reality I witnessed. But I must try.

The first thing I laid eyes on after my reunion with loved ones was the magnificent gate of heaven towering behind them. It was set in an immense wall that extended beyond my sight vertically and horizontally. The gate was made of a pearlescent material, shimmering with iridescent pastel colors that danced as if alive. Though the gate was enormous, the entrance through it was so small that it would admit only one person at a time.

Through the gate I could see a single street running straight through the city. The street was paved with pure gold, but unlike gold, it was transparent like ice. On each side of that street I saw structures—mansions apparently—all richly ornate and breathtakingly beautiful. Above these structures on a high hill shone the brightest light I've ever seen. It would have been too bright to look at on earth. I believe that is where the Lord resides, "high and lifted up." I wanted to climb up that hill and say, "Thank You for letting me be here," but I never got the opportunity.

In heaven, communication is vastly improved over what we experience on earth. Here, we often misunderstand each other. But in heaven, we are given a precise language and the ability to use it so that each word is weighted with specific meaning that cannot be misunderstood. When someone says "I love you," for example, you know all the fullness of the statement. What's more, people in heaven speak only in declarative sentences. There are no questions, because everyone already knows all they need or want to know.

Among the wonders I experienced in heaven were the sounds. Surprisingly, my most vivid memory of heaven is the music. Nonstop melodies filled the atmosphere the entire time I was there. I've never heard anything on earth that came even remotely close to that glorious sound. The most remarkable thing about it was that hundreds of songs were performed simultaneously, but the composition was so precise and the words so articulated that I could make out each song individually. The vocal and instrumental components were perfectly blended, to the point that I was not always sure which was which. Interspersed within the melodies were joyous musical exclamations of praise: "Hallelujah!" "Glory to God!" "Praise to the King!" I don't know whether this music came from angels or humans, but it filled my soul with unspeakable elation.

Even now I sometimes hear echoes of that music. I cherish those heavenly sounds, and I can hardly wait to get back so I can hear them again. The music included many familiar songs, as well as others I had never heard—hymns of praise, ancient chants, and modern-sounding choruses. I didn't hear songs such as "The Old Rugged Cross" or "The Nail-Scarred Hands." There were no songs about Christ's suffering and death—no reminders of sadness or pain of any kind. Why would there be? All of that is finished in heaven, so there's no reason for remembering it.

Time does not exist in heaven either. I've heard it said that this means all activity there is contained in one eternal moment, a concept that tends to portray time's absence as somehow static and immobile. But that is not what I experienced. Events in heaven occur in a linear fashion just as they do within time. The difference is that there is no sense of rush or urgency, of aging or lost time. All eternity is always available for all activities.

As Jesus told His disciples, He has gone to prepare a place in heaven for us, and He is coming back to take us there. He is a carpenter, and He is building heaven now. It's presently under construction. As I stood before that magnificent gate and gazed in awe at that light-bathed hill, I longed to go on into heaven. But apparently my mansion is not yet ready, and I had to come back here. I can hardly wait to return.

Wrestling with Questions about Heaven

One question I often hear is, "Is heaven a real place?" Yes, I can assure you, it is.

Before my experience in heaven, I thought perhaps John's descriptions of heaven in Revelation were symbolic. I don't think that anymore. John gives literal descriptions of a place that is solid and real. Those pictures we see of ghostly people aimlessly wafting about, wearing nightshirts and halos, are sheer nonsense. Heaven is a physical place for physical beings like you and me.

Many Christians—maybe even most Christians—think heaven is a "spiritual" place, by which they mean it exists in some kind of ethereal or vaguely immaterial mode. In their minds, if a place is spiritual, it must have a ghostly existence; it's not as substantial as the physical world we inhabit.

People think this way because they grossly misunderstand the meaning of *spiritual*. *Spiritual*, as used in the Bible, means one of two things: under the dominion of God's Spirit, or inhabiting a parallel dimension invisible to us. The fact that heaven and angels are invisible to us does not mean they are less real or less solid. Clear glass, too, is invisible except for its edges and the reflections on it, yet we don't question its reality.

The idea of a less-than-substantial spiritual realm seems to have originated with Plato, and Platonism has little in common with Christianity. Plato asserted that there is a non-physical, non-corporeal world of spirit that is greatly superior to the physical world we inhabit. His philosophy gave rise to Gnostic heresy in the early days of Christianity and influenced a number of early theologians whose erroneous thinking lingers with us today. The Bible affirms in several ways that the physical world is not inferior to the spiritual world, and that the spiritual world is not immaterial. If it was, why would God have gone to such great lengths, and endured such enormous suffering, to redeem the physical creation that He pronounced to be good?

Another thing people often want to know is what we will do in heaven. Persistent popular images of heaven picture it as a place of perpetual rest and inactivity; consequently, many Christians are not all that excited about going there.

We all want meaningful activity. We don't want to idle away eternity doing nothing but sitting on clouds, playing harps, and roaming golden streets. That's too much like the men I've known who have retired with nothing to do but golf, fish, putter in the garden, and hang around the house driving their wives crazy. Within months these men were so sick and tired of their life of leisure that they leapt at the chance to do something useful, like volunteer work or getting a part-time job as a store greeter.

Nobody wants a dull, meaningless existence. Well, I can assure you that God has elaborate plans for us that will demand the best of our strength, minds, and abilities. That is the underlying message of Jesus' parable of the talents.

I think the fear that heaven may be boring stems from three errors in our thinking. The first we just dealt with—the Platonic/Gnostic heresy that skews our view of heaven. If the physical creation is evil, and only that which is spirit survives this earth, then our future would look pretty bland, because without bodies, we couldn't do anything. We would have no hands with which to build, no feet with which to move about, no palate to delight in food, no ears to hear great music or the words "I love you." God has created humans to accomplish work by means of a physical body, and without that body, we're incomplete and helpless.

Second, we may fear that heaven will be boring because, perhaps subliminally, we think evil is more interesting than good. That's why we hear jokes about people preferring hell "because that's where all the fun and interesting people will be." That thinking comes partly from the idea that Christianity is a religion of "thou shalt nots," and everything enjoyable is a sin. Good Christians won't dance, drink, watch TV, party, or ever think about sex. Life is stripped of flavor, and the good person is not one who *acts* but one who *avoids*.

Too many Christians have fallen for this lie. Like the two men pictured in a cartoon wearing robes and halos and sitting idly on fluffy clouds. One says to the other, "You mean we spent our lives resisting temptation for this?" Evil is not more interesting than good. Evil glitters on the surface, but it soon deadens the senses. Good, while sometimes seemingly less attractive on the surface, actually leads to real joy and excitement.

One example that shows the contrast is sex and marriage. Free sex without restraints or responsibility looks more exciting than married sex, which binds people to one partner and forces them to make compromises and adjustments in their lives. But it turns out the opposite is true. Studies show that marriage produces happier people who enjoy better sex than bed-hoppers. Bed-hopping leads to repetition, boredom, loneliness, and meaninglessness.

Third, we misunderstand what the Bible means by "rest." Heavenly "rest," biblically speaking, generally refers to relief from the pains and frustrations of this world, not lazing away our days in celestial hammocks. Remember, God gave Adam and Eve work to do in Eden before the serpent ever arrived on the scene. And God declared it "good." It was not until Adam and Eve sinned that work became associated with toil and sweat. So in the perfection of heaven, it would make sense that, just as in the first days of Eden, we would have fulfilling, joy-filled work to do—only without the hardships and obstacles that accompany it in our fallen world.

Some people ask me where heaven is. Is it located somewhere beyond the galaxy? Is it in another dimension? Or could it possibly be here on earth? Determining the location of heaven presents some knotty problems. The word *heaven* appears in the Bible some 400 to 550 times, depending on the translation. The word refers variously to the atmosphere, the sky, the invisible dimension, God's dwelling place, and our future home. To the Jews, *heaven* had seven meanings, each referring to a layer of the air and space above the earth. The first heaven was the atmosphere below the clouds, and the seventh was the place above the stars where God dwells.

The ancients believed God's heaven was up somewhere above

the stars. But since the earth is a spinning globe, "up" depends on what continent you're on and what time of day it happens to be. Many people believe heaven exists in a separate dimension, and this may be true. When the apostle Paul refers to the "heavenly realms," he certainly refers to a dimension coexistent with our own in which beings invisible to us live and move.

Many theologians believe the future dwelling place for humans will actually be a refurbished earth. Highly respected Christian thinkers such as N. T. Wright, Billy Graham, C. S. Lewis, and Randy Alcorn present this view in their work. Various biblical writers, including the prophets and apostles, wrote of a new earth too, which raises the question: if the heaven we're promised is "up there" or in some other dimension, why does God promise a new earth?

Scriptures such as Isaiah 11 address this question by referring to a time when all things will be restored. And the language of Romans 8:18–25 indicates that redemption means complete restoration of God's original intention. It makes sense to think that God would be determined to restore His original creation. Why would He allow Satan victory over what He declared good?

This question of heaven's location is one that confused the apostle Thomas. Jesus said He was going to prepare a place for the disciples and urged them to follow. "Lord," Thomas replied, "we don't know where you are going, so how can we know the way?" Jesus answered, "I am the way and the truth and the life. No one comes to the Father except through me" (NIV; see John 14:1–6).

If the home of the redeemed is a renewed earth, then what and where is the Holy City that John described and I experienced? Revelation 21 explains that after the earth is renewed, the Holy City comes down to it from heaven, and a voice announces that God will now dwell with men. The Holy City is God's capital, to be placed on earth as His dwelling so that He can again live and walk with His people, just as He originally did with Adam and Eve in Eden.

If what we call heaven is really a restored earth, then where did I go when I died for ninety minutes? Randy Alcorn and others believe there is an intermediate heaven where people go before they are finally resurrected. Perhaps that's where I was. It may be that the Holy City I saw is the same city that will be lowered onto the earth when the earth is renewed after its coming destruction.

I did not get a map showing the physical location of heaven, but I do know the way. And so do you. The way to heaven is simply Jesus, who is preparing a place there expressly for you right now if you've claimed Him as your Lord and Savior.

Your task is to prepare yourself. Heaven is real, but that will mean nothing to you if you are not going, and you won't go unless you prepare. Heaven is a prepared place for prepared people.

1. Have you given much thought to what heaven will be like? What impressions are strongest?

2. Look at Hebrews 11:9–10 and notice the contrast between Abraham's life on earth and his future in heaven. What does this say about the reality of heaven?

3. What do you think might be the significance of the small opening Don saw in the gate to heaven?

4. You've read Don's description of heaven. The prophet Ezekiel also attempted to put the glories of heaven into words (Ezekiel 1). What stands out to you about his description?

5. Now read John's account of the City of Jerusalem from Revelation 21. What are the similarities with what Don and Ezekiel relayed? What is most poignant to you?

LIVE WHAT YOU'VE LEARNED

As you go through the coming week, look for hints of heaven around you. Are there moments of pure joy or glimpses of beauty that feel like a taste of perfection? Does a strain of music make your heart long for something more, something eternal? Scripture says that the Lord is drawing us toward Him (John 6:44) and that creation testifies to His presence (Romans 1:20). Pay attention to where you see evidence of the spiritual world around you.

WEEK 4

HEAVEN IS A REAL PLACE

"In My Father's house are many mansions; if it were not so, I would have told you. I go to prepare a place for you."
— John 14:2 (NKJV)

Imagine a person confined within a cave in such a way that he must sit with his back turned permanently to the opening. He continuously sees dark shapes moving on the back wall, sun-cast shadows of real people passing the cave's entrance. Having never seen real people, however, the person in the cave thinks these shadows are the true reality; he cannot imagine anything more substantial. Even if he were to suddenly be released from his dark confinement, the sun's blinding glare would initially cause him to see real people and objects indistinctly—more as ghostly figures, and certainly less substantial than the shadows in his dark cave. The appearance to him would be the opposite of the facts, all because he'd spent his life in darkness.

C. S. Lewis used the term *shadowlands* to speak of this earth. The common misconception is that our present shadowlands are more substantial than the reality—heaven. Such spiritualizing of heavenly realities misleads many people. We are physical creatures created for a physical world. For God to place us in a wispy, ghostly eternity would be like putting a fish in an eagle's nest. It might be a lofty, wonderful place with a beautiful vista, but it's hardly where a fish would want to live.

Jesus is now preparing a solid, physical, permanent, and incredibly real place for us flesh-and-blood humans. He is making exactly the kind of environment where you will feel utterly at home. When you arrive, you will be filled with wonder and delight, because it will seem made-to-order, especially for you. As a matter of fact, it will be.

1. How does face-to-face communication differ from letters, emails, or even phone calls?

2. What difference will it make to be face to face in eternity (1 Corinthians 13:12)?

3. Read Job 8:9 and Colossians 2:17. How does discovering that heaven is more real than earth change your perspective?

This vale of tears

is but the pathway

to the better

country: this world

of woe is but the

stepping-stone to

a world of bliss.

—

Charles Spurgeon

4. Given what is said about the heroes of faith in Hebrews 11:13, 16, what will it mean to have a better home than what we find on earth?

Father, thank You for preparing just for me the home I was meant to have.

DAY 2

WHERE IS HEAVEN?

"Then I saw a new heaven and a new earth, for the first heaven and the first earth had passed away."
— Revelation 21:1 (NIV)

Dick Onerecker and the EMTs attending my accident saw my body lying in the wreckage of a car from the time they arrived at the scene to the moment I was loaded into an ambulance. But in spite of what they saw, I was not there. I was in another place where my senses and mind were actively processing wonders completely removed from the twisted metal. The amazing thing is that both places were real.

This inexplicable division of realities gives rise to the question, Just where is heaven, anyway? Where were my mind and senses actually located while my body was pinned in that crushed mass of metal?

According to the Bible, an invisible heaven exists right now, in a realm we can't see, where God and the angels live. Yet the Bible never explicitly says that humans will "go to heaven." Since the prophet Isaiah, the apostle John, and the apostle Peter all wrote of a new earth, it gives credence to the view that our future home may be an earth restored to God's original paradise.

The Lord knows for sure.

Even I still have plenty of questions about heaven. But this much I do know: we must not let our wondering distract us from the central truth that God is preparing an exquisite place for His people. While I wait to return, I'm simply out to witness to you about what I have seen and heard so you will know that whether our future home is "up there," "over yonder," through a dimensional portal, or on a renewed earth, it is a concrete reality that we must get ready for.

1. If Jesus is preparing a suitable home for you (see John 14:2), what do you expect to find there? What makes a place feel like home now?

2. What is Jesus' prayer in John 17:24? What does "belonging" mean to you?

3. What do Isaiah 65:17; 66:22, and Revelation 21:1 teach about the new heavens and new earth?

We talk about heaven being so far away. It is within speaking distance to those who belong there.

—

Dwight L. Moody

4. What greater question does 2 Peter 3:11–13 focus on? How would you answer it?

Father, all Your earthly delights assure me that wherever heaven is, You will fill my future environment with endless wonders.

65

DAY **3**

HEARING HEAVEN'S MUSIC

"The sound I heard was like that of harpists playing their harps. And they sang a new song before the throne."
— Revelation 14:2–3 (NIV)

Everyone likes music. The catch is that not everyone likes the same kind of music. Human tastes run the gamut. Even in Christian music the variety is wide: hymns, praise songs, spirituals, chants, Southern gospel, Christian rock, and more.

As the universal language, music evokes meanings and emotions that are common to all cultures. Yet somehow, for all its "universalness," music has a lot of dialects! You might think this diversity of tastes would pose a dilemma for God. If He wants music to universally speak to people in heaven, how can He choose one style over another? The music I heard in heaven may be the answer—a perfect blend of many songs of many kinds. That music showed me that God loves beauty, order, variety, and harmony. But here on earth, our diversity sometimes causes "worship wars" that prevent music from being a unifying language among God's people.

Christ tells us clearly in Matthew 5:23–24 to reconcile our differences before we approach God, or else our worship is worthless. So the harmony we should seek in preparing ourselves for heaven is not in our music but in our relationships. It's not found in the country music fan learning to like Handel, or the tobyMac listener learning to enjoy Gaither. It's in loving people more than music and letting others have the kind of music that moves them toward God.

Harmony is the essence of heaven, and the heavenly music I heard there expressed it. Achieving harmony with fellow Christians is one way to begin hearing the glorious music of heaven while we're here on earth.

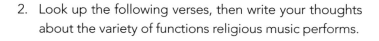

1. What ways are Christians urged to adopt in Ephesians 5:19–20? How can we do this in our daily lives?

2. Look up the following verses, then write your thoughts about the variety of functions religious music performs.

   1 Samuel 18:6

   1 Chronicles 16:7

   2 Chronicles 35:25

   Colossians 3:16

   James 5:13

Music is God's gift to man, the only art of Heaven given to earth, the only art of earth we take to Heaven.

—

Walter Landor

3. What was the significance of Don hearing nothing but songs of praise in heaven? Are other types of songs helpful in our churches now? Explain.

Father, I am happy to know that music will be part of my life in heaven. Please guide me toward harmony with other believers here and now.

WEEK 4

4

WILL I BE BORED IN HEAVEN?

"'Well done, good and faithful servant! You have been faithful with a few things; I will put you in charge of many things. Come and share your master's happiness!'"
— Matthew 25:21 (NIV)

If I thought heaven was the kind of place many people imagine, I wouldn't look forward to going. It's bad enough to be bored on earth! I spent thirteen months flat on my back with nothing to do but memorize episodes of some of TV Land's finest, and it was all the misery I ever want to know.

Interestingly enough, before I experienced heaven firsthand, I thought little about what it might be like. I suppose I had subconsciously adopted the prevailing misconception—that heaven is essentially an elaborate retirement center where we will spend all our time strolling aimlessly with no meaningful work to do and no real contribution to make. Put another way: except for the absence of pain and sorrow, the heaven many of us envision is not that much different from my agonizing boredom in the hospital.

Obviously, there's something wrong with this picture.

The Bible corrects our thinking, saying we are created to be lords of the earth—the title Adam forfeited to Satan. That task will be restored to us. What will we rule? We're not told, but if heaven is a fresh new earth, we will be charged to develop it with our creativity. Cities will need to be built and managed. Those cities will need tradesmen, merchants, contractors, farmers, musicians—virtually every honorable occupation we have on earth. There's every reason to think that those who have found their talents here will use them in heaven. And those who never found the one thing they were best suited for will finally find it there. Bored? Not on your eternal life!

1. How might work in heaven differ from work on earth? In what ways do you hope it will be the same?

2. Which abilities would you love to use in heaven? How might they be useful there?

3. What hints do Matthew 25:23, 2 Timothy 2:12, and Revelation 5:10 give us about our future with the Lord?

4. In Scripture, heaven's *rest* usually means *relief* (such as in 2 Thessalonians 1:6–7) rather than *inactivity*. How does this change your thinking about heaven?

Imaginary evil

is romantic and

varied; real

evil is gloomy,

monotonous,

barren, boring.

Imaginary good

is boring; real

good is always

new, marvelous,

intoxicating.

—

Simone Weil

Lord, I look forward to meaningfully serving You in heaven with every ounce of my ability.

DAY **5**

RESERVING YOUR PLACE IN HEAVEN

"Therefore, my brothers, be all the more eager to make your calling and election sure. For if you do these things, you will never fall." — 2 Peter 1:10 (NIV)

The gate I saw opening into heaven was enormous—wide enough to accommodate throngs of people and so tall I could not see the top of it. Though what surprised me about the gate was that set within it was a smaller door no wider than those leading into my own house. I thought nothing about this narrow door at the time; I was absorbing too many wonders to be bothered with questions. It wasn't until later, after I had returned to my earthly life, that I came to understand its meaning.

Since we don't go to heaven *en masse*, it's not what church you're a member of that gets you there. We enter individually, one at a time, gaining God's presence on the basis of our one-on-one relationship with Him. Choosing God is a personal decision each of us must make. And God loves us personally. In fact, He loves you as if you were an only child. Had you been the only person ever to exist, I'm convinced that Jesus still would have died for you.

God wants to welcome each of us into heaven as if we were the only person entering. That's the meaning of the tiny door. The important question is, are you preparing to enter that door?

Preparing for heaven is a little like packing a suitcase for a journey, or like an engaged woman gathering what she'll need to set up housekeeping with her new husband. In our present life, we are accumulating the attributes that will make us good citizens of heaven. How ready are you?

1. Paul gives us a list of things to pack in Colossians 3:12–14. What's on it?

2. Note what we're told to "put on" (NIV) in Romans 13:12, Ephesians 4:24, and Colossians 3:14.

3. See 2 Corinthians 4:16–18. How are your present difficulties preparing you for heaven?

And, after death,

what cometh?

What wonderful

world will open

upon our

astonished sight.

—

Charles Spurgeon

4. In light of 1 Timothy 6:7, 19, what foundation are you laying for eternity?

5. Write your thoughts about the last sentence of the parable in Luke 12:16–21.

Father, in gratitude for Your invitation to join You in heaven, I promise that I will become more diligent in preparing for it.

ARE ANGELS REAL?

"Are not all angels ministering spirits sent to serve those who will inherit

salvation?" — Hebrews 1:14 (NIV)

Our Invisible Helpers and Comforters

I was speaking in the church where Dick Onerecker was pastor, telling how he had arrived on the scene where my body was trapped in the wreckage of my car. I explained how he had worked his way through the back of the vehicle—the only access possible—and prayed for me, and how much the feel of his hand gripping mine had meant as I was regaining consciousness.

Afterward Dick's wife told me that I wasn't telling the story correctly: her husband never held my hand. I knew he did, because the comfort and strength I drew from his firm grip was the one thing that kept me clinging to life. But she insisted that Dick did not hold my hand. It would have been impossible because of the restricted space in the crushed car and our relative positions. Dick, who was behind the back seat, had had to stretch his arm as far as he could just to place his hand on my shoulder; he could not possibly have reached my right hand, which lay on the passenger side of the front seat.

I knew without a doubt that someone had been holding my hand, and with a thrill, I suddenly realized: it had to have been an angel.

I have always believed what the Bible affirms—that angels are all around us, constantly active in many ways. But I had never had tangible evidence of angels until the day of my accident, both in that moment in the car and during my time in heaven.

Christians today do sometimes question whether angels are still active in our lives. I have never actually seen an angel as far as I know (though according to Hebrews 13:2, I may have seen angels whom I thought were men). But as I've looked back at significant moments in my life, such as one particular night in my hospital room (which you'll hear about this week) and when Dick Onerecker prayed for me, I know beyond doubt that angels were there.

Let me give you three reasons to share my assurance of angels in our lives today. First, we have the same need for their ministry that God's people have always had. We still live in a fallen world where the fog of our sin natures and the evil we encounter put us in dire need of divine help, for we are no match for demonic powers seeking our destruction.

Second, we have God's promises of continuing angelic protection. (Psalm 91:11; Luke 4:10; Hebrews 1:14). Third, we know that angels are active today because we have many credible testimonies of their work among us. In his book *Angels*, Billy Graham relates several incidents where angels protected people from harm or guided them to safety. Other Christians tell of angels warning them of danger, helping them when stranded, and bringing peace to the dying. Some angel stories we hear may be spurious, but we dare not dismiss all accounts, especially those that come from reliable witnesses.

Often in the Bible, angels appeared simply as men, as when they announced the coming birth of Isaac to Abraham and of Samson to Manoah. This is why Hebrews 13:2 advises us: "Don't forget to show hospitality to strangers, for some who have done this have entertained angels without realizing it!" (NLT). At other times, angels have been present but invisible, as when an angel barred the way of the prophet Balaam and an army of angels stood ready to protect Elisha at Dothan.

73

In a few instances, angels have appeared in their spectacular native form, often scaring people senseless, as when the angel rolled away the stone at Jesus' tomb on Easter morning. "His countenance was like lightning, and his raiment white as snow: And for fear of him the keepers did shake, and became as dead men" (Matthew 28:3–4 KJV). If you see a sight like this, you won't have to wonder whether you've seen an angel!

Among the most persistent misconceptions that people have about angels is that we will be angels when we get to heaven. That is not true. Angels are of an altogether different order than humans, though their exact mode of existence is difficult to know. They are equally effective in both the realm we inhabit and the invisible realm that Paul sometimes calls "heavenly" or "spiritual." Their apparent comfort in both realms seems to support what we earlier affirmed in this series: the spiritual realm is not immaterial, but rather a physical reality that is simply invisible to us because it is in another dimension. We call that other realm "supernatural," meaning it is outside the dimension that is natural to us. But to the angels living in that dimension, it is a perfectly natural, solid, and visible environment.

The Bible indicates that there are different orders or possibly ranks of angels, but identifying and defining the heavenly hierarchy is controversial, with theologians differing widely in their claims. We can, however, safely identify three orders of angels: archangel, cherubim, and seraphim. The term *archangel* pretty well defines itself: the prefix "arch" means "chief, head, or greatest." Only one angel is called an archangel, and that is Michael in Jude 9. Many biblical scholars, however, believe that Satan also was once an archangel, equal or even superior to Michael.

The seraphim are mentioned only in Isaiah 16:1–6. The prophet describes them as having six wings but does not mention how they are ranked in the angelic order. The ministry of the seraphim is that of praise to God. If they have a ministry relating to humans, we're not told of it.

The cherubim are mentioned sixty-two times in the Old Testament. A cherub prevented access to Eden after the fall of Adam and Eve, and it is cherubim whose likeness was depicted as spreading their wings over the mercy seat of the Hebrew tabernacle's ark of the covenant. Cherubim are described as having hands, feet, and one pair of wings. Ezekiel saw flying cherubim accompanied by an elaborate wheel within a wheel. Like the seraphim, they are associated with God's glory, but they also minister to humans. We are not told whether they rank higher, lower, or equal to the seraphim. Where we ever got the idea that cherubs were little fat baby angels with tiny wings and curly golden hair is a mystery.

Angels are immortal, eternal creatures designed specifically to be God's servants. Angels have supernatural power subordinate to God's power; they can take on human form; they can enter our dimension and do their work in it as effectively as in their own dimension. We humans, on the other hand, are the only creatures described in the Bible as being created in God's image. We are mortal and subject to death. Even in our resurrected state, we will continue to be the humans that God created us to be.

While we're on earth, we are "a little lower than the angels" (Hebrews 2:7, 9), but when we are resurrected, it appears that our positions will reverse. Apparently, angels will answer to us in some way, because we are told that we will judge or rule them in 1 Corinthians 6:3.

Another popular misconception is that all angels are good. No, the Bible tells us that back before the creation of Adam, a great and beautiful archangel of heaven grew proud and led an assault on the throne of God, intending to overthrow Him and rule heaven and earth himself (Isaiah 14 and Ezekiel 28 provide a picture of this). Revelation 12 tells of the war in which Michael the archangel led a force of loyal angels and drove this rebellious angel, Satan, out of heaven, along with his mutinous angels (which we now call "demons").

They were cast down to earth, where they have vengefully determined to undo God's creation and undermine our salvation. As Paul tells us, there is still a holy war going on in the invisible realm between God's angels and those that fell with Satan. And we are the prizes in that war. Our eternal future depends on the outcome (Ephesians 6:12).

The first human targets in that war were Adam and Eve. Satan seduced Eve into disobeying God, and she brought Adam down with her. Their sin destroyed their perfect connection with God and robbed them of power to contend with Satan. So he moved in and took over the earth. Now, with his demonic angels, he is working to ruin the world and draw humanity into the hell prepared for him. Because Satan and his angels hate humans, they induce us to evil acts and tempt us to abuse and twist good for their destructive purposes.

The same kind of temptation Satan used against Adam and Eve is now applied to every human alive. And since we inherited our fallen parents' propensity to sin, we all succumb. Satan and his minions don't appear as evil, nor do most of their temptations. They know better. They can appear as "angels of light" (2 Corinthians 11:14), causing sin to look appealing and giving us easy rationalizations for yielding.

Read Ephesians 2:1–3. It is a grim account of people before they accept Jesus Christ as Lord and Savior of their lives. And in it are some astounding statements about the fallen angel Satan, the prince of the power of the air. Indeed, he is at the root of all the evil we experience. When our sin gave him a foothold on the earth, he loosed all controls over nature and everything went awry. Weeds, rot, storms, accidents, disease, pain, death, envy, pride, hate, lust, greed, gluttony, anger, and other evils became the way of the world. Satan is the root source of all sin and all evil, including my accident, the tragedy of 9/11, all wars, tsunamis, volcanic eruptions, floods, hurricanes, and your little secret sin that nobody knows about. We often hear people blaming God for these evils, but they are none of His doing. He made the world perfect; it was Satan who turned it into chaos.

However, we would be mistaken to think the cosmic war with Satan consists only of resistance against temptation and contending with the havoc of fallen nature. As we've read already, there is a war against evil going on in the angelic dimension. God's loyal angels—the angels who did not fall—are our allies in that war (see, for example, Daniel 10 and Matthew 13:36–42), and they fight in actual battles in order to prevent Satan's demons from doing their worst to us, as well as to minister to us.

Satan and his demonic angels are powerful enemies, and left alone in our fallen condition, we would stand no chance against them. But God's loyal angels who come to our aid are even more powerful. They watch over us like a parent whose child is taking his or her first steps; they're ready to guard and defend us against evil or soften its impact, as they did for Christ when Satan tempted him in the wilderness. They bring encouragement when we lose hope, as the angel did for me in my night of despair in the hospital. Angels are the communications corps who bring messages and answers to prayer from God.

What is your part in this war? Your main task is to resist Satan's temptations and align yourself with God. As James 4:7 succinctly states it: "Submit yourselves, then, to God. Resist the devil, and he will flee from you" (NIV). Of course this means you should stay away from the occult, psychics, séances, and such because such activities open the way for invisible demonic forces to influence you. This is exactly what happened to Saul in 1 Samuel 15.

It's vitally important that you submit to God, learn His will, and adhere to what you know is good. Those who do not learn truth will slide into evil; evil loses its ability to discern truth. That's when we become susceptible to believing a lie (2 Thessalonians 2:9–11). Avoid Satan's deceptions by subjecting your heart, mind, and spirit to God. When you are firmly committed to God, evil will be evident as evil, and you will be given the power to resist Satan and his demons.

The Enormous Importance of Angels

The words *angels* and *angel* appear in the Bible some 286 to 327 times, depending on the translation. Angels appear in every section of the Bible—the books of the law, history, poetry, the Prophets, the Gospels, the epistles, and the apocalyptic books. In each of these appearances, angels are doing God's work on earth. In many cases they do work that is attributed to God. That's what Billy Graham meant when he called angels "God's secret agents." An agent is one who acts on behalf of another, accomplishing tasks in the name of the one he represents. There are times in the Bible when a person who saw an angel counted it the same as having seen God Himself. For example, in that strange story of Jacob wrestling all night with an angel, Jacob explained why he named the place of the encounter Peniel: "It is because I saw God face to face, and yet my life was spared" (Genesis 32:30 NIV).

In addition, they are active in God's presence and on the earth, protecting us and carrying out God's intentions. Billy Graham tells us that there are moments in life when you are surrounded by a legion of angels. They form a hedge around believers for comfort, encouragement, strength, and protection against the assaults of the enemy. These angels are enormously compassionate beings who love us and are dedicated to our welfare. They watch over us, sometimes protecting us from evil or delivering us from some catastrophe. The Bible records several instances of angels appearing to men and women, and we are told that it can happen to any of us (Hebrews 13:2).

They also see us safely through to heaven when we die. We read in Luke 16:22 that when the beggar Lazarus died, "the angels carried him to Abraham's side [heaven]."

The angels we see depicted in popular culture are attractive, non-threatening, and easy to love. Thus, many people pray to angels, look to angels as their guides, and expect to be with their angels after death. In short, some people put angels in the place of God.

The fact is, God's angels do much more than just protect, comfort, and bring good news. They also execute His holy judgment and discipline, as when they brought death to the firstborn of Egypt and pestilence to the Israelites when David disobeyed God by conducting a census. Their role in executing God's final judgment is elaborately pictured in the book of Revelation. His angels are totally committed to carrying out His will and bringing His purposes to completion on this planet. And if it takes discipline and destruction to do it, they stand ready to carry out the task.

And yet what utterly amazes me is that, in spite of these tremendous responsibilities and the difficulties we cause them—in spite of the fact that we are newcomers in God's creation who fell and rebelled against God—they love us. They help us. They rejoice when we turn to God, and they joyously celebrate our arrival in heaven.

Think of it: they have been around longer than we have, and those now in heaven have never sinned but remained loyal to God. They are extremely beautiful and powerful beings dedicated to service, who don't give in to pride, who don't seek status or prestige, who fight battles that are not their fault, who must coddle, baby-sit, and defend weak and sinful humans—and yet they ecstatically celebrate our successes.

If only we Christians would be like that! We have more reason for joy than any creatures in all creation. God wants us to experience joy at all times—and gives us ample reason for it. It's our pride, our expectations, our lack of patience and endurance, our failure to see the big picture of redemption that stands in our way.

Since my time in heaven, I have learned to hold life lightly. I've been through a horrible experience that left me permanently affected physically. But due in part to the way angels have ministered to me, I decided to live in joy. That is what it takes—a decision. Paul made that decision, and he subsequently expresses joy as often and probably more forcefully than any other Bible writer. He uses the words, "joy," "joyful," "rejoice," or "rejoicing" at least forty-three times in his letters, including this ecstatic outburst: "Rejoice in the Lord always. I will say it again: Rejoice!" (Philippians 4:4).

How could Paul be so joyful when he spent half his adult life under the lash, in prison, being stoned, driven out of town, shipwrecked, and threatened with death? The answer is that he knew his destination. That knowledge gave him hope and put his present difficulties in a new perspective. From the day of his conversion, he never wavered from pursuing his goal.

That's the key. Set your affections on things above. Keep your eye on the prize. Draw inspiration from the example of Paul and the angels, and live your life in real joy.

1. If you've ever had an experience that might have involved an angel, describe the situation. How did that experience affect your faith?

2. Do you find it comforting or unsettling that invisible beings are aware of everything we do? Explain your answer.

3. In 1 Kings 19, the prophet Elijah was running for his life from the murderous queen Jezebel. Read verses 3–8. How much of God's work do you think is done through angels?

4. Hebrews 1:3–6 tells us that humans have long been—and wrongly been—worshiping angels. Why is this wrong?

5. In light of Ephesians 6:12, how do you think the angelic warfare in the spirit world affects the affairs of nations? You personally? What can you do to fight back in this war for human souls?

LIVE WHAT YOU'VE LEARNED

Today, be alert to images of angels. You may see them portrayed in art, in figurines, as decorations, in ads, on greeting cards or websites, or in other ways. Each time you see one, note how the angel is portrayed. Write down the ways in which the image differs from what angels are really like so that you can reset your mind to biblical reality.

DAY 1

WHAT DO ANGELS DO FOR US?

"For he will order his angels to protect you wherever you go." — Psalm 91:11 (NLT)

I love the classic Christmas movie *It's a Wonderful Life*. I think Clarence, the inept angel trying to win his wings, is lovable and endearing. But as much as I enjoy that movie, I have to tell you that angels are nothing like Clarence. They are not former humans, and they do not win their wings. The Bible sometimes describes angels as beautiful or magnificent creatures and, well, Clarence does not exactly fit either of those descriptions.

Nor are angels like what you see painted on cards or sculpted in figurines in gift shops. They are not women or fat little babies with wings. They are not to be prayed to, and they do not grant wishes. They are immortal creatures who perform many functions for God. For example, angels deliver God's messages. They told Mary that she would be the mother of Jesus, announced the birth of Jesus to shepherds, and assured women at the tomb that Jesus had risen. Angels also protect us, as they protected Daniel by shutting the mouths of the lions in the den where he had been thrown.

Angels minister to humans in need, as when they assisted Hagar and her dying son Ishmael in the wilderness and delivered the apostle Peter from prison. Angels gave food and water to Christ after His forty-day fast and duel with Satan in the wilderness. They also strengthened Christ after His prayer in Gethsemane so He could face His coming ordeal.

Since angels care about us and are dedicated to God's will, their existence and presence should be a great comfort. They are powerful, loyal, selfless, and utterly committed to ministering to "those who will inherit salvation" (Hebrews 1:14 NKJV).

1. Which angel stories that you've heard or read seem most credible, and why?

2. List as many angelic ministries as you can. Which are comforting to you? Which are frightening? Explain.

3. What can we gather from Nehemiah 9:6 and Colossians 1:16 about the invisible hosts of heaven?

4. What does 2 Chronicles 32:20–21 suggest about angelic ability to protect God's people?

Millions of

spiritual creatures

walk the earth

Unseen, both when

we wake and

when we sleep.

—

John Milton

Father, knowing that You've provided angels as Your eyes, Your hands, and Your voice in our struggle against evil makes me more mindful of Your constant love and care. Thank You.

DAY

2

ARE ANGELS AMONG US NOW?

"For he will command his angels concerning you to guard you in all your ways." — Psalm 91:11 (NIV)

The toughest time of my life was my thirteen months of recovery in the hospital. I can't begin to tell you how terrible it was. I lay flat on my back, unable to move, totally dependent on doctors, nurses, and other caregivers. I had no assurance of recovery, no way to do anything but watch TV. And the pain was horrific . . . constantly. Day by day my emotions sank lower until I was in a real depression. I became sullen and angry, and lashed out at my poor caregivers. Refusing all help, I simply wanted to die.

But one sleepless night my misery came to a head. Feeling everything was hopeless and pleading for death, I asked a nurse to play a cassette tape of Christian songs that I'd never bothered to listen to. Slowly, the music began to speak to my soul, and I felt a strong sense of some caring being there in the room. Soon, to my surprise, I found myself saying, "Praise the Lord!" Then the dam broke and would not stop. I cried for about an hour, until finally a calmness settled over me. I lay relaxed and very much at peace with God and with my situation. My depression had vanished. I had been healed.

As the sun came up, I knew that God had sent an angel to be with me through that dark night, giving me strength and hope—maybe somewhat like the angels gave Jesus on his dark night in Gethsemane. It was a turning point for me, the beginning of the rest of my life. Thank the Lord that He has so elaborately provided for us to be ministered to in our times of need.

1. Why might it be difficult to know whether you have encountered an angel?

2. Read Daniel 10:18–19. What would it be like to be in Daniel's shoes?

3. Read of Paul's situation when he found an angel at his side (Acts 27:23–24). When has your need for encouragement been the greatest?

Angels are the

dispensers and

administrators

of the divine

beneficence

toward us.

—

John Calvin

4. Consider the words of Matthew 18:10 and Hebrews 1:14. Have you ever seen evidence of such a "ministering spirit"?

Thank You, Father, for not leaving us alone in this fallen world. Help me to remember that anyone I encounter today could be one of Your angels.

WEEK 5

DAY

3

OUR STRUGGLE WITH FALLEN ANGELS

"For God did not spare even the angels who sinned. He threw them into hell, in gloomy pits of darkness, where they are being held until the day of judgment." — 2 Peter 2:4 (NLT)

"I've lost my dear daughter, and I can't get over it," the distraught woman said to me on the phone. "Why did such a terrible thing have to happen?"

This poor mother was desperately reaching out for comfort, but I could find little to give because I could not answer her plaintive question.

"I failed her in some way," she continued. Then came several "if only" statements: "If only I had checked on her earlier in the day." "If only I had watched her more carefully." "If only I had monitored her dosage . . ."

I could see that part of this woman's problem was guilt. Though she could not have realistically done anything to prevent her daughter's death, she blamed herself. I've seen it again and again.

When the woman finally told me that her daughter was a believer, though, I found a way to offer comfort: "If she was a believer, she's at peace. She's with the Lord right now." Though I repeated this assurance several times as we talked, it did little good. The mother kept asking "why."

While it's always impossible to know exactly why specific evils happen to people, it's not impossible to answer the question about the beginning of evil in our world. I know the answer to that: it's because of angels.

1. Note the author of temptation's fingerprints in these events:

   1 Chronicles 21:1

   Matthew 4:1

   John 13:2

2. What do Matthew 26:41 and 1 Corinthians 10:13 say about resisting temptation? What help has God provided?

3. Consider Luke 4:13. What does Satan's refusal to give up mean for us?

4. Read 2 Thessalonians 2:9–11 and 1 John 4:1–4. How can Christians avoid being deluded by lies?

Every visible

thing in this world

is put in the charge

of an Angel.

—

St. Augustine

Father, I know that Satan and his demons are going all out to capture my soul. Please open my eyes to see beneath the façade and resist the enemy.

87

WEEK 5

DAY

4

OUR ALLIES IN THE GREAT COSMIC WAR

"For we are not fighting against flesh-and-blood enemies, but against evil rulers and authorities of the unseen world, against mighty powers in this dark world, and against evil spirits in the heavenly places." — Ephesians 6:12 (NLT)

"Of course I'm depressed," the woman said to me. "If you had my troubles, you'd be depressed too."

Before I could respond, she started reciting grievances by rote. When she finished, I asked her several questions. Did she do anything she liked? Did she attend church for fellowship with other Christians? She droned negative responses to my every suggestion.

This woman was clearly a casualty in the massive war Satan is waging against us. The difficulties, setbacks, and evils that assailed her had penetrated her soul and caused her to give up. She was, in effect, Satan's prisoner of war.

I could sympathize because I've been there. Earlier this week I described my own bout with severe depression. Satan came within an inch of taking me prisoner. But a powerful ally came to my rescue and fought off the demonic forces that had darkened my mind. When the sun came up that morning, I knew I was not alone in my struggle.

The war in heaven is not a figure of speech. It is real, it continues even now, and we are participants. In fact, we are the ones under attack—the objective of that war. Our future depends on God's victory. We are told that the victory has already been won at the cross, but Satan has not yet been put away. He fights on with the desperation of a cornered animal. While the ultimate victory is assured, our individual destinies are not; we must each decide whether to join the army of God.

1. Why do we need angelic allies in the war against Satan?

2. Notice the vivid military language used in 2 Thessalonians 1:6–7. What does this passage tell us about the nature of the invisible war?

3. What does Psalm 34:7 say about persevering when evil seems overwhelming?

4. What assurances do you gain from the following passages?

   Romans 7:21—8:2

   1 John 4:4

   1 Corinthians 15:57

   Romans 8:31–32

Few people realize the profound part angelic forces play in human events.

—

Billy Graham

Lord, though I am weakened by my sin nature, grant me the will to depend on Your Holy Spirit more and to grow stronger as a soldier in Your war against evil.

DAY 5

OUR REJOICERS IN HEAVEN

"There is more joy in heaven over one lost sinner who repents and returns to God than over ninety-nine others who are righteous and haven't strayed away!" — *Luke 15:7* (NLT)

I've never felt more overwhelming joy than during those ninety minutes I spent in heaven. I've already spoken of my celebratory reunion with departed friends and relatives and the awesome sights I saw. I've also mentioned the spectacular, joyous music that remains with me even now. Though I never saw who was singing, I have no doubt that it was an angelic choir expressing their praise to God.

In a way, this angelic joy seems quite remarkable to me. Throughout this week, we've explored the many things angels do, from delivering messages to giving aid and comfort, to fighting battles against mighty enemies, to executing God's judgments. Now we find that these extremely busy and powerful warriors have a softer side. They are incredibly talented musicians, capable of performing the most intricate and joyful heavenly music. That is one reason I call angels "God's rejoicers."

In spite of their many tasks, heavy responsibilities, and frightful battles, angels are obviously highly joyful creatures. And they bring their joy to us, as the angel did on my dark night of depression.

If Paul and Silas were able to sing praises while in prison for healing a girl with a demonic spirit (Acts 16:16ff), we can do so in our circumstances too, whether health issues, financial struggles, the loss of a loved one, addiction, envy, or bitterness are threatening to imprison us. When we give God dominion of our lives, our hearts, our attitudes—when we respond with joy in the face of injustice, persecution, and evil—the angels of heaven rejoice. Another victory has been won in the battle for our worship.

1. What reasons do Christians have to be joyful?

2. How are the angels described in Job 38:7?

3. Describe the picture of angels that Hebrews 12:22 offers. Now also read verses 23–24. What do you think are their primary sources of joy?

4. How can you find the same joy in your dark hour that Paul and Silas did?

There's not much practical Christianity in the man who lives on better terms with angels and seraphs, than with his children, servants and neighbors.

—

Henry Ward Beecher

Father, I want to have the kind of joy Your angels exhibit over Your works—the kind of joy Paul and Silas had while in chains. Please make my relationship to You the guiding joy of my life.

DOES HEAVEN CHANGE ANYTHING NOW?

"Above all, you must live as citizens of heaven, conducting yourselves in a manner worthy of the Good News about Christ." — Philippians 1:27a (NLT)

Finding Purpose on the Journey

People often ask me, "If when you left the conference on that January morning you had known that turning right instead of left would lead you to your horrific accident, would you have done it?" My answer is no; I would not willingly put myself through the ordeal that followed. On the other hand, now that it's happened, I would not go back and undo it. The experiences that followed my accident have given me a new perspective on life and a new purpose and direction. And it has changed the way I think and act.

My experience has caused me to ask people this question: "If you knew where you were going, would you act differently on the way?" I fear that most Christians who know that a heaven awaits them do not act as if they were going. They seem sour, complaining, and critical instead of joyful.

I confess that before my accident, my own behavior was much the same. I've told you that as I recovered from the accident I was depressed, angry, impatient, askying God "why?", and wishing for death. Though that all changed the night when music and the presence of an invisible angel broke through my depression, a few years passed before I learned that God had a purpose for me in what I had experienced. Finding that purpose showed me where I am going, and it gave me a new outlook on the journey. The following story will help explain what I mean.

Some time after I was back on my feet, I got a call from a father who told me of his sixteen-year-old daughter, Andrea, whose leg had been horribly shattered in an accident. The doctors wanted to put her leg in an Ilizarov frame, but the girl was resisting it. I went to the hospital to see her. I introduced myself and said, "I wanted to meet you and tell you that I know how you feel."

She didn't believe it until I told her I would have lost my leg had it not been for the Ilizarov frame. I showed her pictures of the device on my leg and explained the process. She listened and asked questions as I encouraged her to wear the device and endure the pain, "because it will be worth it in the end." I prayed with her, gave her my card, and told her to call me anytime, day or night. Then I walked to the door, stopped, turned, and said, "Did you see what I just did? I just walked. I would never have been able to do that had it not been for that device. Without it, I wouldn't even have my left leg. You will walk again too."

Andrea did have the device put on her leg, and she called me every few weeks, sometimes crying in despair. I always listened and gave her what encouragement I could from my own experience. After not hearing from her for a while, I got an email from her mother telling me that Andrea was now walking, and that the device would soon be taken off. She had taken Andrea to the doctor for a routine check, and while in the waiting room Andrea had gone to a despondent-looking man in a wheelchair who was wearing the Ilizarov frame on his own leg. She said to him, "Sir, I just want to tell you that I know how you feel. I've been in this device for many months, but now I am walking, and you will walk again too." She handed him a card and said, "I've written my phone number on here, and I want you to feel free to call me anytime, day or night."

Andrea had learned what I learned. If we know where we're going, we should help others on the way. It makes the trip much better because it gives us a sense of purpose as we journey. Life can shatter us with devastating blows, but God can turn our adversity into a message. As Paul says, as God comforts us, we should comfort others (2 Corinthians 1:3–4). There's no blessing or ministry in hoarding that comfort and letting it stagnate like water in a pond with no outlet.

Partners in the Journey

I might never have helped Andrea if it hadn't been for someone who encouraged me to open up. Long after my recovery, I was complaining to my friend David Gentiles that my life seemed diminished; I could no longer do many of the things I could do before the accident. He probed me until I told him of my ninety minutes in heaven. This was the first time I ever spoke of it.

David showed me how that experience, combined with my experiences with pain, pointed to my new purpose: ministry. Acting on David's advice, I began to share my experience. I was utterly amazed at the response. Thousands of people are in real pain and need hope that they can come through it and find meaning on earth while they are awaiting heaven. People need to know there's purpose beyond tragedy; that heaven is real, making suffering worthwhile. And they hear that message better when it comes from someone who "gets it."

As my story helped others, it also helped me. The reality of heaven gave me a new sense of what is real and what is important, as well as new meaning in my relationships. And to this day, I am enjoying the journey to heaven much more than I ever did before my accident.

How should the assurance of heaven change the way we live?

For one, it offers us joy in spite of our circumstances. At some point we all must learn that happiness and joy do not depend on our situation. Joy is always a decision. Always. Sometimes things happen to you, and from that moment on you'll never be the same. No matter how severe the loss, you have a choice: you can be either bitter or better. It's up to you to decide which. After all, it's not the circumstance that destroys your happiness; it's how you respond to it. I call it "taking a test and turning it into a testimony; taking a mess and making it a message; taking disappointment and turning it into divine appointment."

Heaven also changes the way we live now by reorienting our desires and priorities to what has eternal value. This doesn't mean abandoning our stewardship of temporal things but rather, ensuring that our primary desires and investments (of time and resources) are not self-serving and temporary. Yes, in today's world you need a house and a car, and it's prudent to make retirement plans. But when the house and car become objects of pride and status rather than being mere shelter and transportation, your values have tilted from the eternal to the here and now.

Since experiencing heaven, that "stuff" has lost its importance. I no longer care about the size of my house, the make of my car, the labels on my clothes, or whether I'm judged to be a successful pastor. All these are short-term values that aren't worth my time, thought, or money. What I value is investing in others—giving, helping, loving, caring. Having glimpsed eternity, I can see that the life of every person is eternal. Therefore, investment in others is eternal.

Most people become seduced by the here and now, as if the "near" is more important than the long term. Thus, they pursue immediate satisfactions, settling for temporary substitutes rather than what they truly long for. At some point, though, everyone finds that the things we pursue on earth don't satisfy our deepest desires. The fortune is never enough. The trends of fashion change. The career eats you up and robs you of your family. Each sexual encounter becomes like all the others—the scratching of an itch with no lasting meaning. Each earthly promise bursts like a soap bubble once we grasp it, because it is not the real solution. Earth's pleasures are as elusive as the wind.

The solution is to shift our focus to the real satisfactions that are offered in heaven. With heaven close to our hearts, we can more easily forego immediate satisfaction, social acceptance, and empty worldly pleasures in exchange for the pearl of great price (Matthew 13:45–46).

Martin Luther had that wider perspective. He was once asked what he would do if he knew the world would end tomorrow. He answered, "I would plant a tree today." On the surface, that seems useless. But his point was that if each activity we engage in is the right thing to do at any given moment, then it's what we should be doing, whether our life ends immediately or decades from now. We must plan our lives as if they were eternal, because they are. But we should live each moment as if it were the last, because at some point, it will be.

The assurance of heaven should also motivate us to choose God's will, God's ways, and God's kingdom above all others, including our own. In our humanness we don't always make the right choice, in part because Satan deceives us. He promises a utopian world where we can decide what is best for us and pursue pleasure without limitation. Independence and self-reliance are especially appealing to Americans. In fact, it's part of the fabric of the American spirit. But the truth is, independence is woven into the human spirit as well. It was the desire for independence—the pride-induced idea that we can make it on our own—that caused Adam and Eve to disobey God and that caused Satan's fall. But once we take the bait, the trap springs, and we end up enslaved to sin.

God's way to freedom involves a different path altogether. He created us to be dependent on Him and to joyfully live in intimate relationship with Him under the loving guidance of His Holy Spirit. We like to be strong, independent, and adequate for every task—even the Lord's work. But to receive our Father's "well done," we must allow Him to work through us as the motivating dynamic of our lives. This kind of submission is the only way we'll ever have the strength to stand against the usurper. Our strength alone simply will not cut it.

I thought I was living under heaven's authority before I drove onto that bridge. I lived for God and worked for God. I was one of His men on earth, eager to exert every ounce of my strength to building up His church. In fact, that morning I had a series of sermons on my car seat about being on a mission for God.

I never preached those sermons. They were all about doing for God by our own effort.

That's what Satan lives for. The more we depend on ourselves, the more our self-reliance disconnects us from God and the more vulnerable we become. The way to be under Heaven's authority is to submit to God and allow Him to work through us—a far cry from us taking the reins and working for God.

One of the clearest signs of our devotion to God is to serve each other. And as I've already said, this is what gives purpose to the rest of our journey on earth. Jesus emphasized the importance of service to His disciples, and even went so far as to say there is a real connection between our love for Him, our love for one another, and our final destiny in heaven (see Matthew 25:31–46).

We tend to treat others according to our own whims or needs rather than discerning what they need. But if we could see each person through God's eyes, we would see the truth beneath the surface—not just the hurt beneath the bitterness, and the hunger beneath the despair, but the reality that each of us is created in the image of God. This means that beneath our flawed, aging bodies and fallen souls exists a magnificent being capable of immense glory and joy.

If you want to imagine on some level how God views us, think of the way young lovers look at each other. The young man perceives the girl he loves as the most glorious creature in God's universe. We say he's blinded by love, but actually, it's his love that allows him to see the truth.

What he sees in that rapturous moment is a glimpse of the glory that God has infused into every one of us. It is the truth that will shine forth uncontaminated in each of us when all things are renewed.

The enormous value God puts on each of us is why we must never snub, condescend to, or ignore another person. We must not be rude to waitresses, impatient with store clerks, or angry with telemarketers. We must never condemn anyone, because we don't know his heart or the circumstance that led to her actions. Even when Michael the archangel disputed with Satan, he would not condemn him but instead left the job of rebuking to God (Jude 9).

Our task in this hurtful world is to assist each other at every opportunity, thereby fulfilling our earthly purpose and affirming our citizenship in heaven. There's not one of us who doesn't need help and support in some way, at some time. Our concern and actions on behalf of others display God's love to them. And He loves His people by giving us opportunities to pass along the help and comfort we've received from Him.

1. How can we live a heaven-focused life while dealing with day-to-day necessities?

2. If earth is an extension of God's kingdom, should there be any difference in the way you live here? What should be the same?

3. According to 2 Corinthians 1:3–4, how can our painful experiences be used for others' sake? How does giving comfort put joy into our own journey?

4. How can the words of Colossians 3:1–5 help us deal with tragedy? How should its instruction guide our priorities, spending habits, and schedules?

5. Look at the perspective of the writer's audience in Hebrews 10:34. How much would you be willing to endure for the Lord? What would be the hardest thing to lose?

LIVE WHAT YOU'VE LEARNED

With heaven in view, consider what is temporary and what lasts. Write these categories as column headings on a piece of paper. Then make a list of what you invest your time in during a typical week—people, possessions, activities—and assign each one to the "temporary" or "lasting" category. In looking at the columns, think about what sets the eternal apart and how you can increasingly set the focus of your life on things that will last.

DAY 1

LIVING UNDER HEAVEN'S FLAG

"Do not conform any longer to the pattern of this world, but be transformed by the renewing of your mind."
— Romans 12:2a (NIV)

After speaking in a church in Berlin, Germany, I was sitting at a table greeting people when a woman came toward me on crutches. Seeing how difficult it was for her to walk, I got up and went to her. "I had to come see you," she said.

She was born and raised in East Berlin under Communist occupation. Life was awful: loss of freedoms, strict surveillance, eating rats just to survive. The wall separating East from West stopped at the river, which served as an effective dividing line with armed guards always watching to shoot anyone who tried to swim across.

One day this woman was carrying water along the river when she was overwhelmed by the longing to escape to the other side. She threw down her bucket, plunged into the water, and started swimming. She got about halfway across when a shot rang out. The bullet went deep into her back, and she began to sink. People on the western side jumped into the water and dragged her ashore. Several surgeries saved her life, but her legs were paralyzed. However, she told me, "It was worth it, just to be free."

Like her, we live in enemy-occupied territory that rightfully belongs to God. Satan has claimed the earth and planted his flag. Though we cannot escape until we die, we can be freed from Satan's tyranny by remaining loyal to God and living under His authority.

Remember, we are in God's kingdom, His resistance movement in enemy-occupied territory. Let's live like it, anticipating the day when the war is won and God promotes us to our permanent home in heaven.

1. Share about a time when Satan's "freedom" actually became a form of slavery for you.

2. Why did Jesus die for you (2 Corinthians 5:15)?

3. Read John 14:30–31. What is the key to citizenship in God's kingdom?

4. Reflecting on Hebrews 11:36–38, why is it reasonable to view the earth as "enemy-occupied territory"?

5. Contrast how the world will treat us (Matthew 5:11) with our responsibility toward the world (vv. 12–16). Why do you think Jesus used these metaphors?

We cannot truly face life until we face the fact that it will be taken away from us.

—

Billy Graham

Father, thank You for giving me citizenship in Your kingdom and for the freedom I enjoy in Christ.

WEEK 6

DAY **2**

LOOKING FOR HEAVEN IN THE WRONG PLACES

"Set your minds on things above, not on earthly things."
— *Colossians 3:2* (NIV)

One night after I spoke at a North Carolina church, a female soldier came up to me, sobbing. "I just got back from Iraq," she said. "It was a living nightmare."

I thought she was talking about wartime atrocities; instead, she was devastated about the way she'd lived. "I was raised a Christian," she explained, "but I wanted so much to be like the other girls in the barracks, I just did what they did." That included, in her words, being incredibly vicious to the only faithful Christian in their platoon.

After their platoon returned to the States, the barracks phone rang one Saturday night. "It was the Christian girl wanting me to come to church with her," said the soldier. "I refused with my usual snide insults, but she was undaunted. I was within an inch of giving in, but then some of the girls in the platoon walked in. 'Surely you're not going, are you?' 'Of course not!' I laughed. 'You know you'll never catch me in a church.'"

About an hour later the phone rang again: the Christian girl had died in an accident. "I hung up the phone and dissolved into tears," said the young woman, "and the guilt and grief has been eating me up ever since. But after hearing you speak today, I know what I need to do: I'm going to take that girl's place; I'm going to be the kind of Christian she was."

Everyone on the planet is seeking acceptance, security, and pleasure. Heaven offers all that and more, but sometimes heaven seems remote. Jesus, however, gave us the only lasting solution to our deepest longings: "But seek first his kingdom and his righteousness, and all these things will be given to you as well" (Matthew 6:33 NIV).

1. Can you offer a personal example of giving in to peer pressure? How does the command of 2 Corinthians 6:14, 17 relate?

2. Read Matthew 13:45–46. What might you have to part with to gain something better?

3. What does Christ mean by His reference to the affluent people in Revelation 3:17–19? Why does He advise buying the three items?

4. Look up 1 Thessalonians 5:21–22. What are some of the subtlest forms of evil? How can we test them?

We shall draw from the heart of suffering itself the means of inspiration and survival.

—

Sir Winston Churchill

Father, please strengthen my bond with You so that I will focus on eternal satisfactions rather than empty, earthly ones.

DAY

3

SEEING PEOPLE WITH GOD'S EYES

"If I have a faith that can move mountains, but have not love, I am nothing. If I give all I possess to the poor and surrender my body to the flames, but have not love, I gain nothing." — 1 Corinthians 13:2–3 (NIV)

Not long ago a man came to me and said, "My wife died recently, and I just don't understand why God took her and left me here." Leaving aside the question as to whether God actually "took" his wife, I answered, "I know why you're here: to help everybody else get there."

He asked me what I meant, and I said, "Don't you believe you're going to see her again?" "Oh yes," he replied. "Well then," I said, "you know you're going to heaven, so let's be about our Father's business until that happens. Let's try to fill up that place with people so that they, too, can see their loved ones again.

"Maybe there's another guy out there who's in despair because he lost his wife, and who better than you to sit down with him and say, 'I understand how you feel'? Who can help him better than someone who's been through the same thing? God wants to use your experience with loss to comfort others."

I had no hesitation in telling that man why he was still here because it's actually why every one of us is here. Our task in this fallen world is to help the hurting and lift up the fallen. As Paul says, "As we have opportunity, let us do good to all people, especially to those who belong to the family of believers" (Galatians 6:10 NIV).

1. What does our service to others mean to God? See Mark 9:41.

2. Notice how the following verses encourage us to treat those who don't necessarily share our faith.

   Matthew 5:43–44

   1 Thessalonians 5:15

   1 Peter 2:12

3. Why does the Bible link the love of God with love for others, such as in Micah 6:8 and 1 John 4:20?

We will often find compensation if we think more of what life has given us and less about what life has taken away.

—

William Barclay

4. How are we told to demonstrate our love in 1 John 3:17–18? Why are both ways necessary?

Father, forgive me when I overlook the opportunities You provide to help others get to heaven. Please make my blind eyes see.

DAY **4**

RESETTING TO THE "NEW NORMAL"

"In this you greatly rejoice, though now for a little while you may have had to suffer grief in all kinds of trials."
— 1 Peter 1:6 (NIV)

My accident and the radical measures required to reconstruct my arm and leg left my mobility and function severely limited. Even after I was fully recovered, I could no longer do many of the things I once did. I think these losses hit me hardest when I took a group of college kids on a ski trip. I had always loved skiing, but now I was consigned to sitting in the clubhouse, watching others glide down that beautiful white slope. As I mourned this loss, I thought of a thousand other things I would never be able to do again.

One thing that helped me through this period was reading of a young man who suddenly lost his sight and was compelled by a good friend to make a list of the things he still could do. The young man resisted at first, but finally he gave in, and before long the list had more than a thousand entries. The blind man's outlook noticeably changed as he focused on doing the things he could and chose to ignore the rest.

That's exactly what I need to do, I thought. *Instead of moaning over what I no longer have, I will reassess, discover what I can do, and get on with those things.*

I call my present condition the "new normal." I'm not normal in the way I used to define it, but my present condition is now normal for me.

And the best part of all? Every one of our "can't dos" in this life are only temporary, thanks to God, who will someday make all things new.

1. Have your limitations kept you from some dream? How so?

2. Our losses are temporary because we cannot lose one very important thing. What is that, according to Romans 8:38–39?

3. See Paul's command in Romans 12:15. Recount a time when you experienced this.

4. What encouragement can you draw from 1 Corinthians 15:58?

5. Read 1 Peter 2:21–24. How can you follow in Jesus' footsteps within your own life?

Father, when I am tempted to self-pity, remind me that You will restore all the good things that this world has stolen, and that I already have everything in You.

The ultimate measure of a person is not where they stand in moments of comfort and convenience, but where they stand in times of challenge and controversy.

—

Martin Luther King Jr.

107

DAY

5

HEAVENLY POWER FOR TODAY'S LIVING

"Be still, and know that I am God." — Psalm 46:10a (NKJV)

While I was flat on my back in the hospital, hardly able to move a limb, someone placed a plaque in front of my bed with Psalm 46:10 engraved on it (see above). I thought it was a joke, and a pretty cruel one at that. *What else could I do but be still?* Yet when friends begged to do things for me, my independent streak kicked in and I refused everything—even simple favors like being brought a magazine.

Once I went home from the hospital, I still struggled at friends having to mow my lawn, make house repairs, and stay with me when my wife ran errands. I felt totally unnecessary. Even more so when my poor wife had to go out there and dicker with car dealers to buy a vehicle. She did a great job of it; meanwhile I was flat on my back, having to depend on others for everything large and small.

When my recovery and a straight-talking friend revealed my dependence, that verse from Psalms forced me to hit the reset button. I had never learned to depend on others or on God. I had never stopped long enough to be still in the center of my being and acknowledge who really has the power. Once I did, the Lord taught me how eager He is to share it with those who quiet themselves before Him. And eventually this dependence on God became a new way of life for me.

In learning to lean on God, I found the true source of my strength. In accepting my weakness and calling on His strength, I was beginning to live an earthly life that would prepare me to be in His presence for eternity.

What about you? Isn't it time to declare your dependence?

1. Why do you think we want so much to be self-sufficient?

2. Despite his impressive résumé, what was Paul's assessment of it, according to Philippians 3:8?

3. Where *shouldn't* we place our faith (1 Corinthians 2:3–5)? Where does our real power come from?

4. Who has God chosen, according to 1 Corinthians 1:27? Why? How is this possible?

5. What does Paul mean by his last statement in 2 Corinthians 12:10?

Father, forgive my tendency to do it all on my own. Please remove the pride that keeps me from seeking or accepting help when I need it.

Character cannot be developed in ease and quiet. Only through experiences of trial and suffering can the soul be strengthened, vision cleared, ambition inspired and success achieved.

—

Helen Keller

ARE YOU LONGING FOR HEAVEN?

"Dear friends, do not be surprised at the painful trial you are suffering, as though something strange were happening to you. But rejoice that you participate in the sufferings of Christ, so that you may be overjoyed when his glory is revealed." — 1 Peter 4:12–13 (NIV)

Heavenly Homesickness

When I was involved in youth ministry we took a bunch of kids to preteen camp. It was the first time many of them had ever been away from home, and one little boy began to miss his family so much, he started crying. It got worse through the week, and the other boys began to tease him. One night I saw him moping about, and I went to him and put my arm around him. "It's going to be all right," I said. "Just two more days and we're going home." "I can hardly wait," he said.

I now know how that boy felt. I'm really homesick for heaven, and I can hardly wait to go back. I endure enough pain that heaven offers a very attractive release, and I'm not alone by any means. Paul endured plenty of pain, including some kind of chronic affliction.

He expressed a strong desire to go on to heaven, but as long as he was on the earth he endured and found joy in the journey. God gives the grace to endure and keep on going, but one day the journey will end. I'm ready. I'm homesick for the Kingdom.

The processes of aging and living in a fallen world can make us feel homesick too. Whether or not your body has been ravaged by any kind of trauma, it is certainly diminished in some way by Adam's sin in the Garden of Eden: you have imperfections that affect your health or looks. Some of these imperfections may be severe, as in a deformed limb, a poorly functioning organ, or a chronic disease. But even if your imperfections are hardly noticeable now, age will bring them on and wear you down to a feeble shell of your young self.

In heaven our bodies will be everything God intended them to be when He made Adam and Eve. Paul wrote that God "will transform our lowly bodies so that they will be like his glorious body" (Philippians 3:21 NIV); that is, like the body of the resurrected Christ, the new Adam. That will be a wonderful gift. But what I most look forward to is being forever rid of the sin that has contaminated my life and all of humanity since the Fall and put us at odds with God. No longer will my mind be fogged by uncertainty. No longer will my spirit be tainted by the urge to sin. No longer will my will be persistently inclined toward self. As Paul promised, our restored physical bodies will be raised as spiritual bodies—meaning, as we've pointed out previously, "subject to the Spirit." Thus, our bodily perfection will be accompanied by spiritual perfection (1 Corinthians 15:44).

Longing for heaven puts our focus where it belongs, but there is a danger too: we can become so heavenly minded that we're of no earthly good. When Jesus was taken into heaven, the disciples who witnessed the event were told to quit looking up and get on with the Father's business. Our task is to find a happy balance between knowing where we're going and having a meaningful ministry while we're here.

Some time ago I was asked to speak to a couple of hundred people at a grief support meeting. Everyone in the group had lost a loved one in that calendar year. I told them of the reality of heaven and about how all the loved ones who greeted me at the gate were people who had helped me get there.

Afterward, one woman who was extraordinarily upset wanted to speak with me. She had recently lost her eleven-year-old son, Travis. She had lived a very hard life with her dysfunctional family, recounting in vivid detail addictions, abuse, alcohol, and other horrors I won't repeat. She didn't even know who was the father of her son. One night she decided she had to leave that home, so she just put Travis in her car and started driving. Some lights in the distance turned out to be a church, and she was drawn inside. The sermon moved the woman to give her heart to Christ that night. Travis also became a Christian.

They had not attended the church long before some of the boys invited Travis to a birthday party. The hosts had a pool, and no one quite knows what happened, but somehow Travis slipped out in the middle of the night and drowned.

I assured the grieving mother that Travis was in heaven, but that was not what was bothering her. "Mr. Piper," she said, "you told us that when you got to heaven, you were surrounded by people you'd known all your life who had helped you get there. We didn't know any Christians before Travis became one. I'm afraid he got to the gates and there was no one there to greet him."

I'd never thought of that before, but I put my arm around her and said, "Ma'am, Jesus wouldn't leave Travis alone at the gates. He would come out and get the boy Himself. I can just see them walking into heaven together: 'Welcome home, Travis. I've been waiting for you.'"

I'm homesick for heaven, but when I think of women like Travis's mother, I realize how much work we have to do. There are so many people out there with unspeakable hurts and needs—and countless individuals who have never met Christ. I can't wait to go back to heaven, but meanwhile, I want to take as many people with me as I can. I think that's why we're all still here.

Motivators toward Heaven

People understandably have trouble seeing why God would bring pain, grief, and suffering into the lives of good people. The first answer to the question is that pain is not God's fault, and He doesn't cause the death of anyone. He hates death; He hates sorrow and suffering. These things are with us as the result of human choice to follow self instead of God.

From the moment Adam and Eve pushed God out of the driver's seat, the human organism went out of control. As Jeremiah said, "It is not for man to direct his steps" (Jeremiah 10:23); we were made to be directed by God. But in order for that freedom to be authentic and to be preserved, God had to step back and let Adam and Eve choose. Their choice gave Satan entrance, so he moved in and inflicted pain, evil, sorrow and death upon us. Now these evils strike both the righteous and unrighteous (Matthew 5:44). But because God loves us and wants us to be reconciled to Him, He puts pain to use for our good when it does strike. He uses it as a form of discipline (Hebrews 12:6)—to show us the result of our folly, or redirect us when we go astray; He uses it to motivate us to show compassion toward others; and He uses it to cause us to long for heaven's relief.

Pain can penetrate even the shell of complacency. Like the "ribbing" at highway's edge that jolts our attention when we drift off the road, pain rouses us to the danger of becoming too comfortable in this fallen world—a condition that I fear describes many Christians today.

Advertisers rely on two highly effective motivators to get people to buy: fear and desire. Those TV close-up shots of big, juicy hamburgers create desire, while little thirty-second dramas about families who've lost everything because they had the wrong insurance create fear. Either will drive us to action.

Those same two motivators can cause us to long for heaven. Fear of pain and loss lead us to want heaven as relief. Desire, on the other hand, leads us to want heaven for its own sake. Yet we can't set our desires on things above when we're in love with the life we have here. I am convinced that this is one reason God allows Christians to experience pain. It provides a reality check that shows us this world ain't "it." God says, in effect, "I'm going to allow enough pain in your life to keep you from being lured away by the world's baubles."

We Americans are well acquainted with baubles. We have so much that most of the poorest among us are better off than the majority in Third World countries. As a result, our desire for heaven has been blunted. In fact, we have reached the point where our society as a whole now gives little or no attention to spiritual matters or heavenly values.

With Christian faith no longer a driving force in American life, it takes that much more commitment and backbone to be an authentic Christian. Today, those who insist on living by biblical values are beginning to experience mild persecution, mostly in the form of marginalization and ridicule, but increasingly in more virulent forms. A valedictorian's address is barred because she credits her success to God. Hospital chaplains are fired because they pray in Jesus' name. A beauty contestant is savaged by the press because she endorses the biblical definition of marriage. Christian professors who believe in creation are denied tenure. Unchurched parents disown their newly converted son . . . These are only a few of thousands of such incidents, and according to many observers, it's getting worse.

The need to stand against an increasingly immoral and hostile culture is why Christian community is so important. Christians must commit to meeting regularly at churches. We must choose godly friends who share our values. We must be diligent in exposing our families only to wholesome entertainment and activities. We must monitor what our children are taught in school. We must even be willing to sacrifice economically to ensure more time and involvement with our kids.

Cultivating a taste for heaven is good, but it is meaningless unless we live our lives here in a way that gets us there. When culture threatens to overwhelm you or lure you into adopting its values, it's time to reach deep into your heart, decide where you are going, and commit to facing down all obstacles that stand in your way. That may even mean reordering your family calendar so that the frenzy no longer drowns out God's voice. When we don't hear Him in the whispered pleasures of life or in the murmurs of our conscience, He will resort to the shout of pain to break through.

Our eternal destiny depends on our relational connection with God and our utter dependence on Him. It means giving up our illusions and being face to face with the realities of this broken life. When complacency with an agreeable world or the rising noise of perpetual activity strains that relationship, we can be grateful that God loves us enough to pick up the megaphone and shout a warning. Then, with our focus reset to heaven, we can develop a real longing for the prize that is set before us (Philippians 3:13–14)—a place where sorrow and tears cannot reach.

As you've been witness to throughout this study, my experiences with pain and heaven itself gave me both motivators: fear and desire. However, since most people have not directly experienced heaven as I have, their desire may be weaker. How can you desire what you haven't experienced? The answer is to pick up on the echoes and shadows of heaven that we have on earth, such as nature's beauty and the delights of relationships.

I cherish the earthly glimpses of heaven that God provides, for at times I feel very burdened about the mission I've taken on. Part of it is the emotional stress of sharing in the lives of people who are enduring terrible suffering. Ever since I went public with the story of my ordeal and experience in heaven, I have been flooded with requests to speak all over the world. Now I spend most of my time traveling, speaking, and answering emails and letters from hurting people. Another part of the burden comes from dealing with a heavy travel schedule while coping with my own continuing pain.

But God is good to me. He keeps me joyful by occasionally opening the doors of heaven a bit and letting its light brighten my journey. Sometimes that light shines in through a particularly inspiring time of worship. Or an email telling me that some person has come out of the darkness of grief and feels the rays of God's love. When those moments come, I am "there" again. I re-experience the joy of my time in heaven and long to be there with all my heart and soul. The anticipation grows so strong that I want nothing more than to be in God's presence, relieved of my pain and imperfections and reveling in joyful fellowship with my loved ones.

Some religions would cite my longing for heaven as a weakness, if not a sin. For example, the dominant goal of the prominent Eastern religions is to rid yourself of all desire and reach a point where you long for nothing. But our problem on earth is not that we have desires; it's that we try to satisfy them in wrong ways. Christianity teaches that desire is the motivating force of our lives. In fact, the central longing planted in every heart is the desire for relationship with our Maker. The happy thing about this desire is that God feels the same way about us. He desires fellowship with us so much that He was willing to die to have it (John 3:16).

The love that compelled Jesus to die to get us back is the same love that created a perfect Eden to be our home. When we ruined that home, He promised to prepare it again, and that's what He's working on now. Like Eden, that home is being made expressly to fit us perfectly. Far from being a place of no desire, heaven will be a place of intense desire. Desires will not be taken away; they will be amplified, properly directed, and utterly fulfilled in exactly the way they were meant to be. And when we get there, when we finally arrive in heaven, we will feel that we have arrived at home. We will know that it's the very place we were always meant to live.

1. What are the "glimpses of heaven" that stir your desire for your future home? What renews your appreciation for them?

2. Why do you think even Christians find it so difficult to long for heaven? What daily concerns tend to take priority for you?

3. Which of earth's two motivators is preferable in your opinion? Can the less preferable motivator lead us to the more preferable one? Explain.

4. If you'll look at Job 2:9, you'll see that not everyone who experiences pain turns toward God. What makes the difference? How can we avoid the reaction of Job's wife?

5. Have you ever felt the kind of longing for heaven that Paul describes in Philippians 1:21–23? Why or why not?

LIVE WHAT YOU'VE LEARNED

Take some time today to assess just why you should want to go to heaven. Get two sheets of paper and make two lists. On the first list, write all the difficulties you will be glad to leave behind on earth. On the second list, write all the things you anticipate having in heaven. Let the first list guide the second. That is, for each item you want to be done with on earth, try to replace it with its alternative on the second list. After you have finished, use the "looking forward" list to impress on your mind what you will gain in heaven.

WEEK 7

DAY 1

HOW PAIN POINTS US TOWARD HEAVEN

"Though outwardly we are wasting away, yet inwardly we are being renewed day by day." — 2 Corinthians 4:16 (NIV)

Shortly after I began to speak on my experiences, I received a stinging email from a woman telling me about the death of her daughter. The girl had overdosed, and her death had left the mother extremely angry. Her life was paralyzed, her faith had shut down, and her relationships with other people were ruined.

I wrote back and sympathized with the woman's loss. It was terrible. I told her that my own experience with extreme, long-term pain had caused me to question God's goodness, and I explained how I had come around to understanding the meaning of suffering. We continued to exchange emails, and over time the woman seemed to make progress, though it was slow.

Then, one day I got a call from her. She was very excited. "You'll never guess what happened," she said. "Last night we convened the first meeting of a new program I've started. It's a support group for families of drug overdose victims." She added, "Not only that, but they voted to name the group after my daughter."

Our biblical, theological answers do address the reasons we experience pain, but they are not the answers people hear when they are suffering deeply. They need comfort, not theology. The best comfort is for them to know that someone is with them in their suffering. And that's where God really shines.

He loved us so much that He came down from heaven and suffered with us, even to the point of bearing extreme torture and a horrible death. He knows pain, and He doesn't like it any better than you do. That's why He invites us all to heaven, where pain and sorrow are banished forever.

1. Why do we resort to blame (especially toward God) when bad things happen?

2. Which of your past experiences make you sympathetic to people in need? (This may be a possible avenue of ministry!)

When Christ

calls me Home

I shall go with the

gladness of a boy

bounding away

from school.

—

Adoniram Judson

3. Since sin entered the world (see Romans 5:12), what do we need to be wary of according to 2 Corinthians 11:3? How can such a thing happen?

4. What does Philippians 2:7–8 say about Jesus' understanding of our pain? What comfort is in this passage?

Father, thank You that You entered this world and suffered with us out of love.

WEEK 7

DAY 2

PAIN IS "GOD'S MEGAPHONE"

"Do not make light of the Lord's discipline, and do not lose heart when he rebukes you, because the Lord disciplines those he loves." — Hebrews 12:5–6 (NIV)

I was at a book signing in South Carolina when a big, burly man with a prominent scar on his face came through the line, wanting to tell me his story. He was raised in a Christian family, and his parents did all they could to instill faith. But when he left home, he determined never to set foot on church property again. His family prayed and pleaded with him to come back to God, but he ridiculed them for using religion as a crutch and said, "The only way you'll ever get me in church again is in a casket."

He nearly got his wish. The man lived a rough life on the road as a truck driver, and one night he fell asleep at the wheel and had a bad accident. He suffered several wounds, including a serious laceration on his face, but he managed to crawl out of the wreckage. When he came to his senses, he found that he was on the lawn of a church. He looked at the truck, wondered how he had survived the wreck, and took the fact that he was standing on church property—where he had determined never to set foot again—as a sign from God. He has been a faithful Christian ever since.

C. S. Lewis wrote in *The Problem of Pain*: "God whispers to us in our pleasures, speaks in our conscience, but shouts in our pains: it is His megaphone to rouse a deaf world." Just as the truck driver discovered, pain can put us back on track when we veer from the path to heaven. Let's be thankful that God sometimes uses a megaphone we can't ignore.

1. Why do we often fail to hear God's voice until suffering makes it loud and clear?

2. What does Revelation 3:19–20 suggest should be our response to Christ's knock? What's your tendency?

3. See Hebrews 12:5–6. How can pain be evidence of God's love? In hindsight, when has the Lord shown you His love in this way?

We can stand affliction better than we can prosperity, for in prosperity we forget God.

—

Dwight L. Moody

4. What are you suffering right now? How can you hold fast to the truth of Romans 8:18 in your situation?

Father, if You must use pain in my life, please give me the wisdom to apply it for Your purposes.

DAY 3

PAYING THE PRICE FOR HEAVEN

"Blessed are you when people insult you, persecute you and falsely say all kinds of evil against you because of me. Rejoice and be glad, because great is your reward in heaven."
— Matthew 5:11–12 (NIV)

I was speaking at a revival meeting in Sweden, and after the altar call two young girls walked down the aisle with a teenage boy who was obviously of Middle-Eastern descent. The young man had been convicted by the message, and said he wanted Jesus in his life. He confessed his belief and joyfully accepted the Lord that night.

As I prayed for the young man, I noticed a large puddle of water on the floor. When the prayer was over, I looked up to see if the roof of the tent was leaking. It was not. That puddle was the young man's tears. He was distraught because his life was in danger simply for attending a Christian meeting. His family was certain to disown him, and they might even kill him for making a commitment to Christ.

He was paying a high price to become a Christian. "But it's worth it," he said. "Knowing my eternal destiny is worth more to me than my earthly home."

We in America take religious liberty for granted, but there are many places in the world where one risks his or her life to be a Christian. And there are many countries where Christians have restrictions on what they can preach and publish.

Unless we develop a real longing for heaven and a taste for eternal things here and now, society or family pressures will sweep us along with the cultural tide. We must fix our eyes firmly on the goal, determine to live by an altogether different standard, and then endure against the tide to reach our destination.

1. Has anyone ever said that you stand out from the crowd? Was it in a way that surprised you?

2. In John 15:18–19, what did Jesus mean by saying that we do not belong to the world? Why does the world react to us as it does?

3. What is the command of Romans 12:2? How do we accomplish this?

4. Referencing Matthew 10:36–38, explain how even family members can become "enemies" when one turns to Christ.

If we really think that home is elsewhere and that this life is a "wandering to find home," why should we not look forward to the arrival?

—

C. S. Lewis

Father, make me strong in my faith so that I will stand firmly on Your side and endure any ridicule that comes my way.

WEEK 7

LONGING TO BE PERFECT

"When this corruptible has put on incorruption, and this mortal has put on immortality, then shall be brought to pass the saying that is written: 'Death is swallowed up in victory.'"
— 1 Corinthians 15:54 (NKJV)

My poor body today is a far cry from what it was before the accident. Then, I was healthy and active. If I twisted my back or bruised myself, it healed quickly. Now, it's an entirely different story. I can no longer ski or play ball with my boys. My arm movement is so limited, I have trouble getting change in the drive-thru. I used to love kneeling down to talk with little kids at church, but now I have to sort of bend over. My arm and leg have enormous scars where skin has been grafted like patches on torn jeans. When I walk down stairs—which I must do with extreme care—my knees creak as if they need a shot of WD-40. In short, the wreck left my body a wreck.

In heaven I anticipate having a pain-free, fully functioning body. I expect to be able to play touch football with my family on the lawn of my heavenly mansion, swim in my Olympic-sized pool, and ski down those snowy heavenly slopes like an alpine champion. Whether I actually do any of these things in heaven, I expect to have a restored and beautiful body *capable* of doing them—a body perpetually healthy and vigorous, and no longer subject to sickness, pain, or trauma.

Mostly, I look forward to the day when my mind and spirit will be perfect. Our entire being will be completely, willingly, and joyfully submitted to the Spirit of God, just as it was originally supposed to be. No smidgen of that old desire to sin left in us. That is what I really look forward to.

1. Name some earthly imperfections—including yours—that you anticipate being corrected in heaven.

2. Sum up Romans 7:22–25 in your own words.

3. According to 2 Corinthians 5:17, what has already happened to us? When will we see this work completed?

I am still in the land of the dying; I shall be in the land of the living soon.

—

John Newton

(on his deathbed)

4. Describe your emotional response to the promise in Philippians 3:20–21. How does it affect your hope? Your sense of peace? Your joy in the journey?

Lord, I am sorry that I have this persistent impulse to follow my own desires. Help me to continually fight with the power of Your Spirit until the day I'm no longer impeded by sin.

125

DAY 5

HOMESICK FOR HEAVEN

"For to me, to live is Christ and to die is gain."
— Philippians 1:21 (NIV)

God draws us toward Him by tantalizing us with glimpses of the nature of heaven. We see it in the love we experience, in the beauty of creation that still shines through the damage of the Fall, and in the delights of our God-given senses.

Heaven is the only place in God's creation where all desires will be fulfilled and all needs met. It's the only place where we will be able to exercise our abilities without obstruction. It will be a place of extreme beauty, extreme love, and extreme delight to all the senses.

As I have often said, heaven is a prepared place for prepared people. But I sense that more people believe in heaven than are preparing for it. I urge you not to be one of those people. Don't let the world sidetrack your desire. Don't let fear of death stop you from focusing on the glory that comes after the grave. Don't just live in the now; live ahead. You have a glorious goal out there. God has a new thing waiting for you, and you don't want to miss it. Doesn't it make sense to begin packing for the trip now?

Peter encouraged: "So, friends, confirm God's invitation to you, his choice of you. Don't put it off; do it now. Do this, and you'll have your life on a firm footing, the streets paved and the way wide open into the eternal kingdom of our Master and Savior, Jesus Christ" (2 Peter 1:10–11 MSG).

I have been homesick for heaven ever since those ninety minutes I spent there, and I can hardly wait to go back. I'm ready. My bags are packed, and my ticket has been validated by the blood of Jesus. I really hope to see you there.

1. What is the purpose of desire? How can it harm us? How does it help us?

2. Read Colossians 3:1–2. What differs in focusing your mind versus your heart? Why are both important?

Sometimes God has to put us flat on our back before we are looking up to Him.

—

Jack Graham

3. Reference 2 Timothy 4:7–8 and Philippians 1:21–23. Is your longing for heaven as strong as Paul's? Are you as prepared?

4. In the last seven weeks, how has your perspective on heaven changed?

Father, in my best moments, I do want heaven more than anything in this world. Please increase that desire, and make it so strong in my heart that it leads me home to You. Amen.

127

WEEK 1 NOTES

WEEK 2 NOTES

WEEK 3 NOTES

WEEK 4 NOTES